Y'SHUA

Y'SHUA

by

Moishe Rosen

MOODY PRESS

CHICAGO

Unless otherwise indicated, all Old Testament passages are
quoted from *The Holy Scriptures According to the Masoretic Text,*
Copyright 1917, 1945, The Jewish Publication Society of America.

Other Old Testament quotations are from *The Holy Scriptures
According to the Masoretic Text: English Version Translated and
Revised by Alexander Harkavy,* Copyright 1916, Hebrew Publish-
ing Company.

All New Testament quotations, except those noted otherwise, are
from the *New American Standard Bible,* © 1960, 1962, 1963, 1968,
1971, 1972, 1973, 1975, and 1977 by the Lockman Foundation,
and are used by permission.

Library of Congress Cataloging in Publication Data

Rosen, Moishe.
    Y'shua.

    Bibliography: p. 127.
    Includes index.
    1. Jesus Christ—Messiahship. 2. Bible. N.T.—Relation to
the Old Testament. 3. Judaism (Christian theology) 4. Jewish
Christians. 5. Apologetics—20th century. I. Title.
BT230.R67 1982   232'.1   82-14349
ISBN 0-8024-9842-6

25 27 29 30 28 26

Printed in the United States of America

Dedication

To the many Jewish people who have wondered, and to the few Jewish people who have asked the question: Can Jesus be the promised Messiah of Israel? God's answer to that question and longing is to be found in one word, a name. That name will be honored above every other name, and eventually every knee shall bow and every tongue shall confess the name of Y'shua.

"And thou shalt call his name Y'shua, for he shall save his people from their sins."

Matthew 1:21
(literal translation)

Contents

Preface

Traditions! Life is full of them! Families have traditional recipes; national groups have traditional holidays. Even in our private lives, most of us have traditional ways of dressing, traditional routes we take to work, and perhaps most important of all—traditional ways of thinking.

When it comes to the topic of religion, most people either shy away from the subject or express a traditional viewpoint that has not necessarily been thought out. Many Americans, for instance, hold to a vague traditional belief in God, with the hazy idea that what God really wants from all of us is that we behave nicely and enjoy life.

Perhaps no group has been as immersed in tradition as the Jewish people. Through centuries of persecution, through times of being tossed from one country to the next, tradition has been the glue that has held us Jews together. Among Jewish traditions there is probably none so firmly ingrained and as little thought about as the one that says Jews are not supposed to believe that Jesus is the Messiah.

You may ask, as did Tevye in *Fiddler on the Roof*, "Where did this tradition come from?" And typically, you will get the response that Christians have persecuted the Jews. Indeed, memories of the Crusades, the Inquisition, the Pogroms, and the Holocaust are imbedded deep within the Jewish psyche. Yet, every Passover serves as a reminder that anti-Semitism did not begin with Hitler, or the Czar, or the Popes. Anti-Semitism goes back beyond the time of Pharaoh and is as old as the Jewish people themselves.

No, the issue is not that of persecution. Rather, it is quite simply whether Jesus is the Messiah of Israel. If He is, all Jewish people should believe in Him, as should the rest of those who would serve God.

But traditional beliefs and prejudices do not die easily. Several years ago while I was in London for a visit, I took a stroll in Hyde Park, a sanctuary and platform for speakers of every ilk. Anyone there can announce and proclaim anything he likes in relative safety.

I stopped for a while to listen to one man perched on a ladder because he was talking about Christianity. He was an atheist who insisted that no shred of evidence existed to verify that Jesus had ever lived. "Have you ever stopped to consider," he asked rhetorically, "that the Jews, who were eagerly looking for a Messiah, never took Jesus seriously? Why not, I ask you? They didn't then, and neither do any today. I know of not one single Jew who ever believed Jesus lived, died, and rose again!"

I never like to heckle public speakers; I'm too often in that position myself. Still, I couldn't let this pass without comment. So I called out from the crowd, "Hey, mister, may I climb your ladder?"

"What's that?" he asked.

"I want to climb up on your ladder."

"What on earth for?" He looked genuinely puzzled.

I took a deep breath. I wanted to be sure everyone could hear me. "I want this crowd to see what you claim you've never seen. *I'm* a Jew who believes that Jesus lived, died for my sins, rose again, and sits at the right hand of God in reigning glory!"

At first his face reddened. But then he got control of himself. "Why, my good man," he said, "I don't mind at all. I can tell by your accent that you're an American. I'm sure all the people here would be delighted to behold you." He smiled sarcastically as he descended the ladder.

Meanwhile I moved my large frame—I'm six feet two inches tall and I weigh about three hundred pounds—up to the front and climbed to the top of the ladder, where I tottered precariously. My host assumed the role of a sideshow barker. He bowed grandly to the crowd and introduced me—he'd asked me my name before I went up the ladder—as Mr. Moishe Rosen, an oddity from America.

Before I had to endure much of his acidic commentary, however, another voice from the crowd broke in. "Hey, up there, do you have another ladder?"

"My good chap," the atheist called back, "what do you want another ladder for?"

The voice called back with a strong British accent, "I want it because my wife and I are Jews, and we also believe that Jesus is the Messiah, that He lived, died, and rose again—and He is our Lord. We think the crowd ought to see us, too. But there's not nearly enough room for the two of us to join that big man atop that little ladder!"

The crowd burst into laughter, and the atheist's balloon burst with it, for the man's preconceptions clearly did not square with actuality.

Long ago, the Jewish Scriptures predicted the coming of One who would redeem the world from evil and usher in a new order of living. This book examines those prophecies to see whether Jesus fulfilled them. If He did not, we Jews should reject Him. And since those same Scriptures also tell us that it is the duty of every Jew to bring the knowledge of the true God to the world, if Jesus is a fraud, we owe it to our Christian friends to expose Him and to help free them from their deception, just as the London atheist tried to do.

If Jesus is not the Messiah, Christianity is merely the concoction of liars or fools, another of the world's plethora of religions that should be immediately dismissed for being far too otherworldly, for making us weak in the face of our enemies, and for depriving us of the free and uninhibited enjoyment of the sensual pleasures of life. If it's all *naarishkeit* (foolishness), Christians are on a path to nowhere; they have deposited the treasures of their lives in a bag full of holes.

But as Tevye also said, "on the other hand—" Suppose the Christians are right? What if Jesus really *is* the Messiah? A debate over whether the tomato is a fruit or a vegetable may not be of much consequence; but whether Jesus is the Messiah, a deceiver, a lunatic, or the figment of someone's imagination—*that* is a question that will affect us both here and now and for all eternity. For if what Christians have been saying for two thousand years turns out to be right, we owe it to ourselves, to the world, and especially to the God of Israel to believe in the Messiah whom He has sent. At the very least, we should be willing to examine the evidence to see if it's so.

If you're willing—turn the page.

Acknowledgments

This book is as much the work of Rich Robinson and Dennis Baker as it is mine. The research and the writing were shared by several. Zhava Glaser deserves special credit for her work on the indexes.

Yet together we agree that no one deserves any particular credit for telling the truth. For us, it is a duty, although not one which is unpleasant. Sometimes the truth has made us uncomfortable, but we remember the words of one who said, "Ye shall know the truth, and the truth shall set you free."

Introduction:
All About the Messiah
(and Everyone Else)

THE TERM

Before we talk about who the Messiah is, it's important to understand what the term meant to Jewish people from the earliest days up through the time of Jesus. So let's begin with a look at the kaleidoscope that is the history of the Jewish people before the year 70 C.E.

The word *Messiah* is the English transliteration of the Hebrew term *mashiach*, which means "anointed." Originally it referred to the way a person (usually a prophet, king, or priest) was designated for an important position by smearing or anointing him with oil in what was the ancient equivalent of a swearing-in ceremony. In time "anointed" came to be used as a synonym for the prophets, the kings, and the high priests themselves. It emphasized the fact that God had designated them for their office. That is why David, for example, although he became an adversary of King Saul, took great pains to see that neither he nor any of

---

* See Appendix 9 for an explanation of terminology.

1

his followers inflicted physical harm on the king because he was the Lord's "messiah," translated "anointed" (see 1 Samuel 24:7).

THE HISTORY

HERE COME THE BABYLONIANS AND PERSIANS

When Nebuchadnezzar* and his Babylonian armies captured Jerusalem in 586 B.C.E., the Temple was destroyed and the monarchy was swept away. When the exiles finally returned to the land some seventy years later, they were subjects of a new empire, that of the Persians. Although they could rebuild their Temple and install a new high priest, there was no hope of placing one of David's descendants on the throne. That God's anointed would again come and restore Israel to her rightful place of honor and glory became only a dream in the hearts of the Jewish people.

THREE'S A CROWD

About 170 years later, Alexander the Great* overthrew the Persian Empire (as you can see, this was a rather busy part of the world) and Israel had still another overlord. When Alexander died in 323 B.C.E., his vast empire was divided among his generals into three parts.

Macedonia, part of Greece today, came under *Antigonid* rule. The *Seleucid* kingdom was the largest part, extending across much of present-day Turkey, Syria, Iraq, Iran, Pakistan, and Afghanistan. The Seleucid capital was in Syrian Antioch near the eastern shore of the Mediterranean. The third party, the *Ptolemaic,* was firmly established in Alexandria, Egypt, and from there ruled Libya, the southern islands of the Aegean Sea, Lycia in southwestern Turkey, Cyprus, and Palestine.

About a century later, however, the Seleucid king, Antiochus III,* captured Palestine and set the stage for further developments.

THE TEMPLE VIP'S

During the three centuries between the return of the exiles from Babylon (538 B.C.E.) and the conquest of Antiochus III (201-198 B.C.E.), the high priests in Jerusalem were the most important and influential members of Jewish society. By then the Jews were well scattered throughout the world, but nearly all of them still paid serious homage to the Temple in Jerusalem. Their offerings poured into it, and even non-Jewish rulers bestowed valuable gifts on this prestigious sanctuary and granted tax exemptions to its priests. Consequently, the high priest had both wealth and prestige, so much so that many coveted his office. But it was a hereditary position, passing from father to son, until the conquest of Antiochus III brought that policy to an end. Thereafter the high priesthood became a prize to be seized by intrigue or violence, or sold to the highest bidder. Under Antiochus IV* (Epiphanes), the Seleucid government took an active and profitable part in those proceedings. The rightful high priest was forced to flee to Egypt; thereafter the office in Jerusalem was filled by a succession of men who seem to have been more concerned with winning and keeping the favor of the Seleucid king than with looking after the interests of their own people.

As a result of the hellenizing influence of the high priest there developed a serious conflict between Jewish religion and Greek ideals. One of the chief ways to gain the coveted royal favor of Antiochus IV was to promote the spread of Greek culture and civilization. The idea was to turn Jerusalem into a city modeled after Athens or Sparta. Although the process of hellenization had been going on all over the Near East ever since the conquests of Alexander, its progress had been slow among the Jews.

Why that was so was understandable. Ever since the dawn of their history, Jews had suffered considerable displacement. After the consolidation of their holdings in Canaan, where they remained for about 700 years, they again suffered displacement, resettlement, and almost constant harassment from neighbors and distant empires. The single constant cord that ran throughout their history was their religion. They worshiped a God who claimed to be the sole Creator and Lord of the entire universe. He was no local deity. Though He might be peculiarly associated with Jerusalem, that was entirely to accommodate His people. There was no escaping Him, no matter where one went. And above all, it was His grace and power that had held the Jews together against all odds.

Consequently, there was intense interest in the whole record of God's dealings with Israel. The canon of the Jewish Scriptures had been gradually determined since the time of Ezra and Nehemiah (c. 450 B.C.E.) as the laws, histories, prophetic oracles, and other sacred writings were brought together into one collection.

Judaism was taking further shape, too, in the emergence

of the synagogues as local places of worship in addition to the Temple and its rites. Synagogues began to be established everywhere around the Mediterranean as places where a devout Jew could join with others of like mind to offer praises and prayers, and to hear the Scriptures read and explained.

Jews experienced an unusual unity among themselves. It transcended national feelings and went back to that sense of God and His calling of them to be His chosen people. They were not just compatriots; they were brothers. This ideal called for intense mutual loyalty, empathy, and dedication.

Taking all this into account, we can see that the typical loyal Jew—and there were many of them—with his God-given law, his God-ordained destiny, his pure worship, and his happy relationship with his fellow Jews, felt that he had nothing to learn from the Greeks in the realms of religion and morality. The way that the upper-class Jewish people in Jerusalem flirted with Greek culture and aped Greek fashions infuriated him.

THE HANUKKAH STORY

The conflict culminated in 167 B.C.E. when Antiochus Epiphanes instituted a program to fully hellenize Jewish religion. He decreed that the God of the Jews would henceforth be regarded as a local manifestation of Zeus, the supreme Greek deity, later known to the Romans as Jupiter. The rites of the Temple and the services of the synagogue would be altered accordingly. To observe any Jewish law or custom that might contravene this new policy would be punishable by death, and many Jews did, in fact, suffer

5

martyrdom. The ultimate insult was the decision by Antiochus* to sacrifice a pig on the altar of the Temple, thus desecrating it and showing his unbridled contempt for the Jews and their God.

Public outrage was soon fanned into open revolt by an aged priest named Mattathias. Three of his sons, the famed Maccabees* Simon, Judah, and Jonathan, carried on the revolt with considerable success, thanks partly to dynastic struggles in the Seleucid capital in Syria. Politics distracted the Seleucids from giving serious attention to the Jewish uprising. The Jerusalem Temple was liberated by the Maccabees and rededicated in December, 164 B.C.E., the event we commemorate today as Hanukkah.* From the next Seleucid ruler, Alexander Balas, Jonathan was able to wrest recognition for himself as high priest. He first exercised that office publicly at the autumn feast of Sukkot* in 152. Upon his death, Jonathan's brother Simon took his place, and by the spring of 142, the Jewish state was relatively independent under his rule. Simon assumed civil as well as spiritual headship, a position to which his descendants fell heir. Simon's grandson, Alexander Jannaeus, took the title of king, as well as high priest. Thus was established the Maccabean or Hasmonean dynasty, which ruled somewhat precariously from 152 until 37 B.C.E., when Herod the Great* took over. During the heyday of Hasmonean power and prestige, some people in Israel were ready to believe that a Messiah—an anointed individual in whom were crystallized the hopes of the nation—had come in the person of this reigning dynasty.

Unfortunately, disillusionment came quickly. The descendants of Simon Maccabee became so absorbed with

the pursuit of power that they betrayed the original aspirations of the Maccabean revolt. Their dynastic quarrels,
incompetence, and misgovernment opened the way for
Roman hegemony, which had been spreading steadily east-
ward for some time. Finally the weakened Hasmoneans
called on the Roman general Pompey for aid. He entered
and occupied Jerusalem in 63 B.C.E. No independent Jewish state was to exist again in this territory for 2,011 years.

PHARISEES AND SADDUCEES

The period of the Maccabean dynasty is notable for the
emergence of two parties in the Jewish community that
were destined to play an important part in the formation of
Rabbinic Judaism and in the early history of Christianity.
Those were the Pharisees and the Sadducees.

The Sadducees, a small group of wealthy and influential
men, occupied the highest religious and civil offices in
Israel under the leadership of the high priest. They had a
reputation for being brusque in manner, harsh in judgment,
and stiffly opposed to any political, social, or theological
change. They particularly disliked certain of what they considered "new" doctrines espoused by the Pharisees: for
example, that the world's evils could be explained by the
conflict between God and Satan, or that the dead would be
raised to live in a future life, and that all would be
rewarded or punished in that life according to their behavior in this one. The Sadducees recognized no binding
authority in religious matters apart from the Scriptures.
They therefore rejected the commentary of the Pharisees.

Proportionately the Pharisees were a small group, but

their cohesion and identity did not depend on wealth, numbers, or position. Instead it was due to their rigorous standards of faith and conduct. Though they were few, their influence on the general population was enormous. The Pharisees saw a divine purpose at work in history and believed God had revealed that purpose in Scripture and in the traditions of Israel. They attributed delays in the fulfillment of the purpose of God to evil spiritual forces that would eventually be defeated. At this final defeat, loyal Israel would be vindicated by God, and the heathen empires would be replaced by a kingdom ruled by the anointed of God, the Messiah of the Davidic dynasty. Men and women throughout Israel eagerly watched for any sign that might suggest that the coming of this Anointed One was near.

HEROD THE HATED

But what signs they saw did not offer much promise. Once the disorders that accompanied the death throes of the Hasmonean line subsided, Herod the Great* came to the throne under Roman patronage. No one could possibly mistake this half-Idumaean, half-Israelite—the embodiment of cunning, violence, and ruthless ambition—for the Lord's Messiah. The Herodian reign bore no resemblance to the Pharisaic ideal of the kingdom of God. Herod reigned from 37 until 4 B.C.E.; the Gospel of Matthew reports that shortly before his death, Jesus was born.

Herod's domain, like Alexander's had been, was divided by his three surviving sons. Archelaus* inherited Judea and Samaria, which today is middle and southern Israel; Antipas,* known as Herod in the New Testament, received

Galilee and Peraea, or the equivalent of modern northern Israel and the westernmost regions of modern Jordan; and to Philip* were allotted territories lying northeast of the Sea of Galilee, part of modern-day Syria. The rule of Archelaus was so oppressive that the Roman Emperor deposed him in 6 C.E. and put his territory under a Roman governor who worked in cooperation with the high priest and the Sanhedrin.* Philip died in 34 C.E., and Antipas was deposed in 39. From the years shortly after Archelaus was deposed, there came a Jewish writing entitled, *The Assumption of Moses.* Its verses reflect how disillusioned the Jews had been by the later Maccabean rulers; how they detested the rule of Herod and his sons; how they resented Roman domination; and how ardently they hoped for the day when God would overthrow their oppressors and establish His chosen people in a position of unassailable supremacy.

THE MEANING

"POPULAR MESSIANICS"

This last description gives a fair idea of how the man in the street might have defined the word "Messiah" in Israel along about 30 C.E. Originally from the Hebrew *mashiach,* the word for Messiah made its way into Greek in two forms. *Messias* was the Greek transliteration of the Hebrew sounds, from which we get *messiah.* On the other hand, the Greek word *christos* translates the meaning of the Hebrew anointed, and comes into English as *Christ.* The word "Christian," then, is equivalent to "Messianist," a follower of the Messiah. It becomes apparent that Gentiles who believe in Christ are really following a Jewish religion!

9

The Messiah, then, was an ideal figure who embodied the hopes of the godly, patriotic Jew of the time. He would be a descendant of David and Solomon. He would be uniquely wise and knowledgeable, upright, courageous, and patriotic, loyally devoted to God. God's power would back Him, and God's wisdom would guide Him so that He could overthrow Israel's enemies and establish God's kingdom of justice, truth, and peace, wherein the Jewish people would worship and obey the one true God, and enjoy permanent prosperity and happiness.

That, basically, is what the Messiah was in the minds of those who were looking for Him when Jesus appeared on the scene. We can now turn to examine His messianic claims, and consider how the biblical vision of what the Messiah would be like differed from the popular conception. We will do this by looking closely at those passages in the Holy Scriptures that Jews throughout history have recognized as messianic prophecies.

1
"O Little Town of Bethlehem"

Few small towns are as well known around the world as one that sits on a hillside about five miles south of Jerusalem. If it were not for the fact that Bethlehem is the birthplace of Jesus, it would today be a place of little prominence. Yet even before Jesus' time, Bethlehem held an important place in the history of Israel, because it was the home of King David's family. The book of Ruth, which tells the story of how a Gentile girl became David's great-grandmother, is set mainly in Bethlehem.

Its associations with David are numerous. It was his home,[1] and the place where Samuel anointed him to be king.[2] A Philistine garrison was stationed there.[3] It was the home of Elkhanan[4] and the burial place of Asahel.[5] King Rehoboam fortified Bethlehem in the late tenth century;[6] Jeremiah, Ezra, and Nehemiah all mention it in their

---

1. 1 Samuel 17:12, 15; 20:6, 28.
2. 1 Samuel 16:1-13.
3. 2 Samuel 23:14-16.
4. 2 Samuel 23:24.
5. 2 Samuel 2:32.
6. 2 Chronicles 11:6.

records.[7] But the most unusual mention of it is found in the book of the prophet Micah, who hails it as the birthplace of the Messiah:

> But thou, Beth-lehem Ephrathah,* which art little to be among the thousands of Judah, out of thee shall one come forth unto Me that is to be ruler in Israel; whose goings forth are from of old, from ancient days [Micah 5:1].

Like all the prophets, Micah knew that the Messiah would be a descendant of David. It is not surprising that the Messiah would be born in Bethlehem, David's city. But what *is* surprising is that Micah declares that the Messiah existed *before* his birth in Bethlehem. The Targum* Jonathan, an Aramaic paraphrase of the Scriptures dating from approximately the second century C.E., renders the passage, "he whose name was mentioned from before, from the days of creation." Raphael Patai, formerly professor at Hebrew University in Jerusalem, remarks, "The concept of the preexistence of the Messiah accords with the general Talmudic view which holds that 'The Holy One, blessed be He, prepares the remedy before the wound.' "[8]

So a primary qualification for the Messiah was that He had to be born in Bethlehem. Jesus seems to fit the bill nicely. The writers of the New Testament record the birth of Jesus as taking place in Bethlehem in a rather unusual manner.

Matthew explains that "wise men" (really a class of religious officials from Babylonia or another Eastern country) came to Jerusalem from the East with the curious announcement that they had seen a star in the heavens that

---

7. Jeremiah 41:17; Ezra 2:21; Nehemiah 7:26.
8. Raphael Patai, *The Messiah Texts* (New York: Avon, 1979), pp. 16–17.

signified the birth of the king of the Jews. Herod was rather troubled and inquired of the chief priests and scribes—those who knew the Scriptures—where the Messiah was to be born. Promptly and unhesitatingly they replied, "In Bethlehem of Judea," and cited Micah's prophecy to back up their assertion. Panic-stricken, in a frenzy of carnage, Herod undertook the slaughter of every male child in Bethlehem under the age of two, in an attempt to kill the rightful heir to the throne. But Jesus' family, learning of the plot, hurried to Egypt and took sanctuary until the danger was past (see Matthew 2:1-18). That may sound like a good plot for a melodrama, but it is history.

There is more. Have you ever noticed that Jesus is called "Jesus of Nazareth" and not "Jesus of Bethlehem"? Nazareth is a northern city in the Galilean area of Israel. Bethlehem, on the other hand, is down in the south. The parents of Jesus lived in Nazareth, but the Romans, who were the de-facto rulers over Israel, decided that the time had come to take a census and that everyone had to return to his place of family origins to be counted. Since Joseph was of the house and lineage of David, he and his pregnant wife Mary had to travel from their residence in Nazareth down to Bethlehem, the home of David. Interestingly, a petition for tax relief from the Jews to Caesar Augustus* delayed the census for a period of time, so that Mary came full term while they were still in Bethlehem.

If anyone might have suspected that the family of Jesus had somehow arranged to have Jesus born in Bethlehem and so fulfill the prophecy about the Messiah's birthplace, this account should make it clear that far from being prearranged, the circumstances were totally out of their hands. However, there is still another part of Micah's prophecy that the New Testament touches on elsewhere as well: the statement that the Messiah was to be preexistent. Matthew's gospel reports this conversation with the Pharisees:

> Jesus asked them a question, saying, "What do you think about the Christ, whose son is He?" They said to Him, "The son of David." He said to them, "Then how does David, in the Spirit call him 'Lord,' saying, 'THE LORD SAID TO MY LORD, "SIT AT MY RIGHT HAND, UNTIL I PUT THINE ENEMIES BENEATH THY FEET" '? If David then calls Him 'Lord,' how is He his son?" [Matthew 22:41-45, quoting Psalm 110].

In other words, the Messiah is a descendant of David, and yet somehow David's Lord, or ruler! Jesus made a declaration similar to this when he told the Pharisees that "before Abraham was born, I am" (John 8:58). Considering that Abraham lived almost two thousand years before Jesus, that's claiming quite a bit! Normally, anyone who talked like that would be considered a lunatic and simply written off as mad. But when they heard Jesus say those things, nobody called him crazy, laughed, or ignored him as we today might treat a babbling derelict in Times Square. Instead, Matthew reports that when asked about David's son, the Pharisees gave no answer to his question—only taunts. Could it be that, knowing what Micah 5:1 and Psalm 110 had to say, they had no answer?

2
Of Snakes and Seed

The story of Adam and Eve is so well known that count-less poems, stories, paintings, and films have drawn on its theme over the centuries. What is not so well known about that story, though, is that it contains a passage that the rabbis have long considered to be the first gleam of a prom-ise that God would send a Messiah. The curtain has barely risen on humanity when the familiar scene occurs: God commands that a certain fruit should not be eaten; the serpent tempts Eve; she eats the fruit and gives some to her husband as well. At that point the Lord pronounces judg-ment on them all, beginning with the serpent, to whom He says,

> Because thou hast done this, thou art cursed above all cattle, above every beast of the field; upon thy belly shalt thou go, and dust shalt thou eat all the days of thy life. And I will put enmity between thee and the woman, and between thy seed and her seed; he shall bruise thy head, and thou shalt bruise his heel [Genesis 3:14-15].

At first sight this seems to be an Aesop-like fable explaining why snakes have no legs. But there are certain curious phrases that compel us to probe more deeply, phrases such as "between thy seed and her seed." In bibli-cal terminology, "seed" has nothing to do with what you plant in a vegetable garden. Rather, it refers to a progeny or a group of descendants, as when God later promised Abraham that his seed would be as plentiful "as the dust of the earth" (Genesis 13:16). But if the reference is to countless generations of progeny locked in battle, why do we read "he" instead of "they"? Could this be a veiled hint of a special individual to come? Is it a promise that the forces of evil unleashed by the serpent would someday be fatally destroyed by this unnamed "he"? In other words, could this be more than just a quaint description of how men dash the heads of snakes underfoot and how snakes most often inflict damage near the feet?

There is something else here that strikes the reader as odd—at least it would if the reader were an ancient Mesopotamian perusing his cuneiform translation of Genesis! It is the phrase "her seed." Biblical society was strictly patriarchal. The generations were traced through sons and fathers, and even today Jews speak of themselves as the seed of Abraham, not of Sarah. So to our hypothetical Mesopotamian, it must have seemed very strange to refer to the seed of a woman.

Both Matthew and Luke in the New Testament provide an explanation. They both claim that Jesus was born while Mary was still a virgin. Biologically that is an impossibility from the outset; but it is amazing that those who will accept the fact that God created the universe out of nothing, won't allow that He could bring about a virgin birth. Nevertheless, the New Testament records this miraculous occurrence as history, and uses an Old Testament prophecy to authenticate it.

Matthew ties the virgin birth of Jesus to Isaiah 7:14, a passage that says, "Therefore the LORD Himself shall give you a sign: behold, the young woman shall conceive and

16

bear a son, and shall call his name Immanuel [God is with us]." The discussion focuses around whether the Hebrew term *almah*, employed here, should be properly translated "young woman" or "virgin." Notice that the sign was to be not only the virgin birth, but the fact that God would be with us. You won't have to be a linguistics expert to understand the following points.

Usually, it is said that if Isaiah meant a virgin, he could have chosen another word, *bethulah*. But *bethulah* could be used of a married woman who was not a virgin, as in Joel 1:8. *Almah*, however, can be shown to mean a virgin in its six other uses in the Hebrew Bible;[1] and when Jewish scholars rendered the Scriptures into Greek during the third and second centuries B.C.E., they translated *almah* in Isaiah 7:14 by the Greek term *parthenos*, which could be understood only as meaning "virgin." That translation represented the best understanding of that day.

Furthermore, we must remember that ancient societies placed a much higher premium on virginity than is customary in our Western culture in the twentieth century. A young woman was assumed to be a virgin unless it was explicitly said otherwise. Besides this, remember that Isaiah 7:14 promised a "sign." An ordinary birth does not seem especially significant as a sign. The evidence points to the fact that what Isaiah is actually talking about, as incredible as it may seem, is a virgin birth. Matthew 1:18-25 tells us that when Joseph discovered that Mary was pregnant, he contemplated a quiet divorce. Although they had not yet come together as husband and wife, in that culture a

---

1. Genesis 24:43; Exodus 2:8; Psalm 68:26; Proverbs 30:19; Song of Songs 1:3; 6:8.

betrothal marked a solemn bonding to each other, so much so that in Jewish law, if Joseph had died before the wedding, Mary would have been considered a widow. God, Matthew continues, had to speak to Joseph directly in a dream to convince him that all was really on the up-and-up. Still, things no doubt looked pretty bad to the neighbors, and we get a hint from John's gospel of the persistence of some unfounded rumors. There we find Jesus rebuking his compatriots, telling them that they were not behaving like children of Abraham and were therefore not his true children. They replied, "We were not born of fornication; we have one Father, even God" (John 8:41). The sarcasm implied that he wasn't one to talk!

But a study of Isaiah would have shown that a virgin birth was not only possible, but was in God's plan 700 years before Jesus was born. Not only was Jesus born in Bethlehem, as the Messiah was to be born, but he fulfilled Isaiah's prophecy about a virgin birth. Maybe some would say that it's coincidental, but it certainly gets one thinking.

3
Fathers and Sons

When Adam and Eve left the Garden of Eden, they didn't exactly get on the next train to the Riviera. Their exit was an exile, and they found life difficult. Ensuing generations continued to display a moral deterioration of such magnitude that God had to send a flood on all mankind, sparing only Noah, his family, and the first zoo in recorded history. But God had made a promise back in Genesis 3:15 (see chapter 2), and He soon took steps to fulfill that promise. He called Abraham to leave his home in Ur* of the Chaldees and to head for the land of Canaan—about the equivalent of God's asking you to take a hike from Philadelphia to Minneapolis. It takes a certain amount of trust in God to say yes to such a venture! Later, when both Abraham and his wife were old and gray, God promised him that all nations would be blessed through him and that his seed (there's that word again) would surpass the dust of the earth in number—something that gave even Abraham a crisis of confidence!

It was thus by a miracle that Isaac came into the world, and God confirmed that the promise of blessing would pass through Isaac and not through any other sons of Abraham.[1] Later still, the promise was reconfirmed as going

---

1. Genesis 17:19.

through Jacob, one of the sons of Isaac.[2] In his old age, Jacob assembled his sons to hear his last will and testament. He announced: "The sceptre shall not depart from Judah, nor the ruler's staff from between his feet, as long as men come to Shiloh; and unto him shall the obedience of the peoples be" (Genesis 49:10). It is interesting to note that a sceptre is the symbolic instrument of a king, not a tribal chieftain. "Shiloh" has been recognized by the rabbis as a title for the Messiah, and Jacob's words as an indication that the Messiah would come from the tribe of Judah.

Can you see how God progressively narrows down the family line of the Messiah? First of all, in Genesis 3:15 Messiah was called the "seed of the woman." At the very least he was going to be a real human being, not an angel or a vague spirit entity. We could have also talked about Genesis 9:27, where the promise goes through the line of Shem, or the Semites. The Messiah could not be Danish, or Ugandan, or Korean. And now, he must be a descendant of Abraham, but not just any descendant. The Messianic promise goes through Isaac, not Ishmael. Then, it goes through Jacob; the Messiah must be Jewish. Next, he must come from the tribe of Judah, which eliminates eleven twelfths of the Jewish people. And finally, we learn that in the family of Judah, the Messianic line goes through King David.

God promised David that his throne would be established forever.[3] And in fact, David's descendants kept succeeding to his throne for four centuries, making them record holders. But even four centuries is not the same as

---

2. Genesis 27:29.
3. 2 Samuel 7:1-17; 1 Chronicles 17:11-12.

forever. We know that no one of David's lineage ever sat on the throne of Judah or Israel after 586 B.C.E. Has the promise been broken or is there a king in the line of Judah today? There are only three possible answers to that question.

The first alternative is to decide that the prophecies were mistakes, not given by God, and useless to tell us anything about the future. The second possibility is that the Israeli Knesset will discover an authentic descendant of David. They will then vote to reinstitute the monarchy, crown the fellow, turn the reins of government over to him, and step down—after all the members of the Knesset have been convinced of the wisdom of such a course. To be honest, it seems more likely that our first alternative was the correct one!

That is, *unless* the third alternative is true. We can examine the claims that Jesus was a descendant of David and that He will actually reign, as 2 Samuel says, "forever." How He could reign for all time is something we'll take a look at later on. For now, though, let's see if He was, indeed, descended from David. After all, if He wasn't, we might as well forfeit all claims that He is the Messiah of Israel.

In John's gospel we find an interesting passage:

Some of the multitude therefore, when they heard these words, were saying "This certainly is the Prophet." Others were saying, "This is the Christ." Still others were saying, "Surely the Christ is not going to come from Galilee, is He? Has not the Scripture said that the Christ comes from the offspring of David, and from Bethlehem, the village where David was?" So there arose a division in the multitude because of Him [John 7:40–43].

21

Matthew (1:1-16) and Luke (3:23-38) each record the genealogies of Jesus. Though they both trace back to David, there is a dissimilarity between them because Matthew follows the line through Solomon while Luke traces it through Nathan, another son of David. It may be that one line traces through Mary (Luke) and the other through Joseph (Matthew).[4] Either way, Jesus' descent from David seems assured.

From Abraham through Isaac, from Jacob through Judah, and from there through the family of King David the messianic lineage was determined. No wonder that when Jesus came to the town of Jericho, a blind beggar named Bartimaeus, hearing him pass by, began to cry out again and again, "Jesus, Son of David, have mercy on me!" (Mark 10:47). There was no doubt whatsoever in Bartimaeus's mind as to Jesus' family tree; he knew, as did the others of that time, that he was indeed a descendant of King David, and an eligible candidate for the title of Messiah.

---

4. Julius Africanus, a theologian of the third century C.E., attributed the differences to the law of levirate marriage by which a widow with no son would marry her deceased husband's brother, that is, her brother-in-law. If she then bore a son by her brother-in-law, the child would be named after the deceased to keep the family name alive. Thus Africanus speculated that Joseph was really the son of Heli, the brother-in-law (as in Luke), but that he took the name of Jacob, Heli's deceased brother (as in Matthew). But as Heli and Jacob were only half-brothers, with the same mother but different fathers, Heli's father traced his lineage to David back through Nathan (Luke), but Jacob traced his through Solomon (Matthew).

4
A Prophet Like Moses

In the history of Israel, Moses stands in a place by himself. He was the great lawgiver, a worker of extraordinary miracles, a prophet of incomparable stature, a man who spoke with God face to face.

God promised Moses that in time to come He would raise up a prophet like him, "and I will put My words in his mouth, and he shall speak unto them all that I shall command him. And it shall come to pass, that whosoever will not hearken unto My words which he shall speak in My name, I will require it of him" (Deuteronomy 18:18-19). Many have claimed to be prophets. And false prophets abound who have claimed this passage referred to themselves. Some interpreters regard this promise as having been fulfilled collectively in the line of such prophets as Elijah, Elisha, Isaiah, Jeremiah, and Ezekiel. Yet, the people of Israel in Jesus' day were still looking for *"the Prophet."*[1] We must conclude that although the passage may refer to many of the prophets, it finds its ultimate fulfillment in some specific, climactic individual who was still being awaited at the time of Jesus.

In the fourteenth century Rabbi Levi ben Gershon wrote: "The Messiah is such a prophet, as it is stated in the

---

1. John 1:19-21; 7:40-41.

Midrash on the verse, 'Behold, my servant shall prosper. . . .' Moses, by the miracles which he wrought, drew but a single nation to the worship of God, but the Messiah will draw all nations to the worship of God."[2]

Indeed, a bonafide prophet had two functions: first, he was to speak the words of God to the people—and that wasn't always the most pleasant task! Isaiah, for instance, launched his writing with a scathing attack on the moral standards of ancient Israel. Balancing this were also words of comfort and consolation. But in each case it was the word of God Himself that was proclaimed.

The second function, and the one usually associated with the word "prophet," was that of accurately foretelling the future. God had, in fact, explicitly warned the Israelites that anyone who predicted falsely was not to be counted as a prophet of God.[3] There were to be no Jeanne Dixons in ancient Israel, right some of the time and wrong the rest of the time; it was 100 percent or nothing, and the prophet's very life was at stake if he was wrong.

Like the other true prophets of Israel, Jesus exercised both functions—forthtelling and foretelling. John the Baptist said that the one "whom God has sent [Jesus] speaks the words of God" (John 3:34). Thus it is not surprising to find Jesus speaking words of rebuke against the moral lassitude of the people.[4] He also uttered predictions, such as the destruction of Jerusalem, which occurred some forty years later in 70 C.E.[5] Frequently the prophets performed mira-

---

2. Rachmiel Frydland, "Messianic Prophecy" (manuscript, 1980), p. 16.
3. Deuteronomy 18:21-22.
4. Matthew 23.
5. Luke 21:20-24.

cles to authenticate their message as coming from God.[6] Jesus also performed miracles.

More specifically, this prophet was to be "like Moses." We recall the Exodus account where Pharaoh, in fear of the Hebrews, ordered all male babies to be killed. But Moses was hidden and escaped. It is striking to compare that story with Matthew 2, where King Herod, fearful lest the Messiah should be born, ordered the destruction of all male babies in Bethlehem under two years of age, while Joseph, Mary, and their child escaped into Egypt.

Then, like His counterpart Moses many hundreds of years before, Jesus emerged from Egypt to provide a redemption for His people—this time not a redemption from physical bondage but redemption from slavery to the power of sin. Moses wandered forty years in the Sinai wilderness; Jesus spent forty days in the wilderness of Judea. Like Moses, Jesus worked various miracles, as a reading of the gospels will show. Consider His discussion with some of the Galilean people in the gospel of John. They asked Him, "What then do You do for a sign, that we may see, and believe You? What work do you perform? Our fathers ate the manna in the wilderness; as it is written, 'He gave them bread out of heaven to eat.' "

To that Jesus gives an astonishing reply: "I am the bread of life. Your fathers ate the manna in the wilderness, and they died. This is the bread which comes down out of heaven, so that one may eat of it and not die. I am the living bread that came down out of heaven."[7] In other words,

---

6. See for instance Exodus 7:10-13; 1 Kings 18:16-39.
7. John 6:30-31, 48-51.

"Though Moses gave you manna, I will give you a better manna—Myself, the source of life."

Moses was a man who worked miracles, led his people to freedom, and spoke God's words as a prophet of God. And yet great as Moses was, there was one greater than Moses to come—Jesus.

5
Forerunner

Every Orthodox Jewish schoolboy trained in the Scriptures knows that before the Messiah appears, a forerunner will precede him like a herald before a king. Thus it is not surprising that Jesus spoke of that prophecy. On one occasion, He brought up the matter of the identity of John the Baptist, that figure whose public activity precedes that of Jesus in the pages of the New Testament. Jesus said that John was he of whom it was written, "Behold, I send My messenger, and he shall clear the way before Me" (Malachi 3:1).

Elsewhere Malachi wrote of the coming of Elijah before the Messianic age.[1] Regarding this, Jesus said, "For all the prophets and the Law prophesied until John. And if you care to accept it, he himself is Elijah, who was to come. He who has ears to hear, let him hear" (Matthew 11:13-15).

Josephus, the ancient historian of Israel, noted that after the time of the prophet Malachi, from about 400 B.C.E., no more prophets arose in the land. It seemed as if God had suddenly become mute. That makes Yochanan ben Zechariah, better known to history as John the Baptist, all the more significant. He was, by the most traditional standards of Israel, a true prophet. Even his emphasis on

1. Malachi 4:5.

mikveh* was not unprecedented. The Jewish people had practiced immersion of Gentile converts to Judaism for nearly a century before John came on the scene. But his use of the ritual was strikingly different. He proclaimed it as an act that signified repentance in preparation for the coming kingdom of God.

Therefore the penitents were baptized to show their conversion* from sin.[2] This rite was administered to Jews as well as to Gentiles.[3] The ethical implications of baptism gained prominence as John reminded the Pharisees and Sadducees to "bring forth fruit in keeping with repentance" (Matthew 3:8). And most important was his announcement accompanying the rite: "Repent, for the kingdom of heaven is at hand" (Matthew 3:2). To receive John's baptism was to turn away from sin in preparation for the approaching kingdom, in expectancy of a mightier one than John who was to come, "I am not fit to untie the thong of His sandals. He will baptize you with the Holy Spirit and fire" (Luke 3:16).

John was a fearless orator, the kind of spellbinder you stop to listen to on a Sunday afternoon in the park. Yet his preaching, with its prominent messianic overtones, represented a serious threat to the security of the local tetrarch or ruler, Herod Antipas, son of Herod the Great.* But John was not content to leave it at that. Herod, you see, had divorced his first wife and had taken for himself his half brother Philip's wife, Herodias, contrary to Jewish law. John, firebrand that he was, proceeded to denounce Herod for his arrogant lawlessness. Herodias was furious. She had

---

2. Luke 3:3.
3. Mark 1:5.

her daughter Salome dance before Herod as a kind of birthday present. He was so pleased that he offered to grant Salome whatever she would ask. With a bit of prompting from her mother, the girl decided that she wanted the head of John the Baptist.[4] This bit of grisly history has long intrigued artists and musicians. It has even been retold in modern symphonic form in Richard Strauss's *Dance of Salome*.

Returning to the Tanach* for a moment, note that Isaiah had prophesied, "Hark! one calleth: Clear ye in the wilderness the way of the Lord, make plain in the desert a highway for our God" [Isaiah 40:3].

That passage came readily to mind for John's contemporaries. John had been preaching in the countryside, literally in the wilderness. Thus the gospel writers called him "the voice crying in the wilderness" (Matthew 3:3), quoting the Septuagint* translation in Greek so common among Jews of that era.

After more than four hundred years of prophetic silence, we can only guess at the impact John made among the people. The gospels report that multitudes came to him, including tax collectors (who were considered to be extortioners), prostitutes, and soldiers. The Pharisees and Sadducees came to watch, and some of them also submitted to baptism. The sense of expectancy, that God was about to do something powerful and dramatic, must have been intense. Luke records that the crowds who heard him questioned in their hearts whether John was perhaps the Messiah. But John spoke of one to come even greater than himself.

---

4. Matthew 14:6-10.

Jesus came down to the Jordan River to be baptized by John, not for the forgiveness of sins but apparently as a means of identifying with those to whom He would soon be preaching. John tried to stop Him, saying, "I have need to be baptized by You, and do You come to me?" But Jesus answered, "Permit it at this time; for in this way it is fitting for us to fulfill all righteousness" (Matthew 3:13-17). After Jesus was baptized, and following a time of testing in the desert, He began His own ministry of teaching and performing astonishing signs and spectacular wonders. News of an especially notable miracle—the raising of a dead man, a widow's only son—reached John's ears. Whether to verify the significance of such miracles, or whether because his imprisonment seemed at odds with messianic expectation, he dispatched two of his disciples to ask Jesus, "Are You the Expected One, or do we look for someone else?" But they did not get an immediate verbal answer. Instead, we read:

> At that very time [Jesus] cured many people of diseases and afflictions and evil spirits; and He granted sight to many who were blind. And he answered and said to them, "Go and report to John what you have seen and heard: the BLIND RECEIVE SIGHT, the lame walk, the lepers are cleansed, and the deaf hear, the dead are raised up, and the POOR HAVE THE GOSPEL PREACHED TO THEM. And blessed is he who keeps from stumbling over Me" [Luke 7:21-23].

What sort of answer was that? Why beat around the bush? But Jesus apparently knew the cardinal rule of all communication: show, don't merely tell. Every speaker knows that he will surely fail to make his point unless he illustrates it memorably. In these terms Jesus' answer could not have been clearer nor more unmistakable. John and

Jesus were serious Jews. They had undoubtedly memorized large sections of the Torah, the prophets, psalms, and other parts of the Scriptures. Thus John would realize that Jesus was performing the sure signs of the Messiah as prophesied by Isaiah. Three brief passages will illustrate:

And in that day shall the deaf hear the words of a book, and the eyes of the blind shall see out of obscurity and out of darkness. The humble also shall increase their joy in the LORD, and the neediest among men shall exult in the Holy One of Israel [Isaiah 29:18-19].

Then the eyes of the blind shall be opened, and the ears of the deaf shall be unstopped. Then shall the lame man leap as a hart, and the tongue of the dumb shall sing [Isaiah 35:5-6].

The spirit of the LORD God is upon me; because the LORD hath anointed me to bring good tidings unto the humble; he hath sent me to bind up the broken-hearted, to proclaim liberty to the captives, and the opening of the eyes to them that are bound [Isaiah 61:1].

Could Jesus have been more explicit?

6
The King-on-a-Donkey

If someone were to ask you to describe the life-style of a king, you would probably think of dazzling palaces, priceless jewels, and for traveling accommodations, either a Mercedes or perhaps an elephant—depending on the country and century you had in mind! The book of the prophet Zechariah also talks about a king, only in rather peculiar terms:

> Rejoice greatly, O daughter of Zion, shout, O daughter of Jerusalem; behold, thy king cometh unto thee, he is triumphant and victorious, lowly, and riding upon an ass, even upon a colt the foal of an ass. And I will cut off the chariot from Ephraim, and the horse from Jerusalem, and the battle bow shall be cut off, and he shall speak peace unto the nations; and his dominion shall be from sea to sea, and from the River to the ends of the earth [Zechariah 9:9].

The Targums* apply this verse to the immediate situation, assigning it no messianic significance because a humble, suffering, and dying Messiah was not acceptable to the Jews of the era in which the Targumim were composed. Yet Zechariah's words bring us to the very heart of the messianic paradox. It is portrayed in the juxtaposition of the words "triumphant and victorious" with the words "lowly, and riding upon an ass." Triumph and victory are traditionally associated with stridency, pride, arrogance, and strutting. Humility, lowliness, and meekness seem utterly out of place in this setting. Yet what shall we make of it in this passage? We may, like the Targumists, seek to modify it in some manner so that it portrays a triumphant figure without the complementary images of suffering and lowliness. But the only honest alternative is to confront all the data as objectively as possible, seeking, when we are confronted by paradoxes such as occur here, to arrive at a portrait that is as unretouched as possible.

Those two aspects highlighted the ministry of Jesus. On the one hand, His ministry was characterized by power and triumph. The miracles and wonders He worked attracted enormous crowds. We read of incident upon incident; and many of them were selected for the record, not merely to show that Jesus was a mighty miracle worker, but because they served to illustrate a spiritual point. Some of Jesus' miracles, for instance, were designed to demonstrate the real meaning of the Sabbath; by healing on the Sabbath, He was able to point out how far the religious leaders had strayed from the true intent of the commandment.

John concludes his narrative of Jesus' ministry by saying, "There are also many other things which Jesus did, which if they were written in detail, I suppose that even the world itself would not contain the books which were written" (John 21:25). We may protest that writers in the ancient Near East were customarily given to hyperbole; yet even in the twentieth-century West, the two largest categories in the Library of Congress are the Civil War and Jesus of Nazareth.

On the other hand, throughout the gospels, and especially at times of greatest public acclaim in response to His teaching and miracles, Jesus often struck a discordant note that emphasized the cost of discipleship in terms of suffering and sacrifice. Most often this note reflected His understanding that, though He envisioned an ultimate and spectacular triumph, He must first go to Jerusalem and there subject Himself to scorn, derision, shame, and death. For example, we read in Luke:

And He took the twelve aside and said to them, "Behold, we are going up to Jerusalem, and all things which are written through the prophets about the Son of Man will be accomplished. For He will be delivered to the Gentiles, and will be mocked and mistreated and spit upon, and after they have scourged Him, they will kill Him, and the third day He will rise again." And they understood none of these things, and this saying was hidden from them, and they did not comprehend the things that were said [Luke 18:31-34].

You probably noticed the title "Son of man" in that passage and wondered what that was all about. We need to examine this title, which occurs in the verses just cited above and very often in the gospels, especially the gospel of Mark.

"Son of man" was a term first employed in Ezekiel. There it seems to be little more than a stylized equivalent of "man." However, by the time of the writing of Daniel and of later, nonbiblical apocalyptic* literature, the term has taken on exalted proportions. For instance, this portion of the book of Daniel is charged with intensity:

I saw in the night visions, and, behold, there came with the clouds of heaven one like unto a son of man, and he came even to the Ancient of days, and he was brought near before Him. And there was given him dominion, and glory, and a kingdom, that all the peoples, nations, and languages should serve him; his dominion is an everlasting dominion, which

34

shall not pass away, and his kingdom that which shall not be destroyed [Daniel 7:13-14].

By the time, then, that Jesus arrived on the scene, it is likely that the title "Son of man" had accumulated a good deal of mystery around it. Jesus applied it to Himself more readily than any other term. He offered no explanation for it, assuming that His hearers would understand. But, as we observed, it often occurs in settings that speak of both Messianic humiliation and exaltation. The term became a kind of verbal "tip-off" that here was somebody who would suffer and die, and yet reign in triumph.

With that as background, we should turn to examine the way in which Jesus chose to enter Jerusalem, as described by Mark:

> And as they approached Jerusalem, at Bethphage and Bethany, near the Mount of Olives, He sent two of His disciples, and said to them, "Go into the village opposite you, and immediately as you enter it, you will find a colt tied there, on which no one yet has ever sat; untie it and bring it here."
>
> And they brought the colt to Jesus and put their garments on it; and He sat upon it. And many spread their garments in the road, and others spread leafy branches which they had cut from the fields. And those who went before, and those who followed after, were crying out, "Hosanna! BLESSED IS HE WHO COMES IN THE NAME OF THE LORD; blessed is the coming kingdom of our father David; hosanna in the highest!" [Mark 11:1-2, 7-10].

We are struck by Jesus' deliberate manner. He is consciously arranging to fulfill Zechariah's oracle. "Aha!" you might say. "Anyone can arrange to fulfill prophecies about the Messiah. I might as well go into the streets and say that *I'm* the Messiah himself!" But don't forget—not only was the Messiah to come riding on a donkey, but He had to have a specific birthplace and a specific family tree, as we've already seen. And we'll look at some prophecies that no one could consciously fulfill. But that Jesus did arrange to fulfill this prophecy says one thing about Him—He believed Himself to be the Messiah. After all, if *He* denied it, why should *we* defend Him? But this is a good indication that we should pursue our investigation.

By the way, "hosanna" is a Hebrew term that means "Save us, we beseech Thee." It comes from Psalm 118:25 which was sung on the holiday of Sukkot,* with the congregation waving *lulavim*, the "leafy branches" of the above passage. In time the term "hosanna" became connected with messianic hopes, and palm branches came to be used at times other than Sukkot (see the apocryphal* books 1 Maccabees 13:51 and 2 Maccabees 10:7, the latter showing their use at Hanukkah). Nobody watching Jesus enter Jerusalem that day could have misunderstood either His intent or the expectation of His followers. They clearly saw from His actions that He was declaring Himself to be the messianic king, riding the donkey of Zechariah. Would further events bear out His claim?

7
A Clockwork Angel

Another prophecy about the coming of the Messiah is even more startling than Zechariah's statement about the King-on-a-donkey. Daniel pinpoints the exact year of the Messiah's coming in the ninth chapter of his book. The angel Gabriel arrives to give Daniel the following particulars:

> "Seventy weeks are decreed upon thy people and upon thy holy city, to finish the transgression, and to make an end of sin, and to forgive iniquity, and to bring in everlasting righteousness, and to seal vision and prophet, and to anoint the most holy place. Know therefore and discern, that from the going forth of the word to restore and to build Jerusalem unto one anointed, a prince, shall be seven weeks; and for threescore and two weeks, it shall be built again, with broad places and moat, but in troublous times. And after the threescore and two weeks shall an anointed one be cut off, and be no more; and the people of a prince that shall come shall destroy the city and the sanctuary" [Daniel 9:24-26].

That passage is difficult to untangle, so let's get to work. The Hebrew word for "week" used in this passage is *shavuah*, which means "a period of seven." It could mean a seven of anything, but here we can understand from the context and the external evidence regarding the entire book of Daniel that the term means a unit of seven years, and that the prophecy deals with seventy times seven years, or

490 years. The word authorizing the rebuilding of Jerusalem probably refers to the edict of Artaxerxes, in about 445 B.C.E. That being the case, 490 years brings us to the first half of the first century of the Common Era. But during the nineteenth century, a British scholar, Sir Robert Anderson, sought to perform much more refined calculations in an effort to pinpoint the intended date. In his book *The Coming Prince*, he explains that a year in Jewish calculations at the time of Daniel was 360 days. With that in mind, let's trace his fascinating exercise.

The Messiah, according to Daniel, will come 173,880 days after Artaxerxes' decree because the 69 weeks of verse 25 amount to 483 years, which we then multiply by 360 days (483 x 360 = 173,880). In this connection, it is better to take the passage as reading 'seven weeks and threescore and two weeks' rather than breaking it up as in the above translation.

The date of Artaxerxes' decree was March 14, 445 B.C.E. because the first day of Nisan (Nehemiah 2:1-6) fell on March 14 in 445, according to the Royal Observatory in Greenwich, England. Anderson figures the imprecise "in the month of Nisan" to be the first day because the Mishnah explains that the first of Nisan "is a new year for the computation of the reign of kings and for festivals."

Anderson sets the day for Jesus' entry to Jerusalem as April 6, 32 C.E. Luke said Jesus began His ministry in the fifteenth year of Tiberius Caesar, whose reign began in 14 C.E. Most scholars agree that Jesus' ministry continued for three years, which brings us to 32 C.E. John (12:1) says Jesus went to Bethany "six days before the Passover" and that He entered Jerusalem the "next day" (12:12). Passover is always 14 Nisan, which according to the Royal Observatory, fell on Thursday, April 10, 32 C.E. Thus Jesus had arrived at Bethany April 4, which was a Friday. His meal with Lazarus at Bethany must have been a Sabbath meal. That means "the next day" could not have been the Sabbath, when Jesus and His disciples would have rested, but instead, Sunday, April 6, 32 C.E.

So, we ask, was Sunday April 6, 32 C.E. exactly 173,880 days from Artaxerxes' decree on March 14, 445 B.C.E.? By counting we can discover that, in terms of the Julian calendar by which we operate, it is 477 years and 24 days. However, we must deduct one year because there was no year "0" between 1 B.C.E. and 1 C.E. That leaves us with 476 years and 24 days which amounts to 173,764 days (476 x 365 + 24 = 173,764).

Leap years add 119 days to that (476 divided by 4 = 119), which brings us to 173,883 days. That is remarkably close to the 173,880 days we figured in Daniel, but not exactly the same. Undaunted, Anderson notes that the Julian calendar is still slightly inaccurate to the true solar year. The measure of this imprecision is 1/128. That is, the Julian calendar year is 1/128 of a day longer than a true solar year. Therefore we omit leap years every 128 years on our calendar. During a period of 483 years, as in Daniel's sixty-nine weeks, there are three such omissions. Hence we may subtract three days from our total and arrive at precisely the same number with which we began, 173,880.

So it is possible to figure Daniel's seventy weeks less one to the exact day that Jesus entered Jerusalem on the back of a donkey. Daniel also speaks of the anointed one's (Hebrew *mashiach*, or *Messiah*) being cut off. The Hebrew term *yikaret* implies a sudden, violent end, which corresponds to Jesus' crucifixion. If it could be self-fulfilling to ride into Jerusalem on a donkey, it is much harder to arrange the exact day—especially if, to be consistent, it means that you'll have to arrange for your own execution as well!

Immediately after that, we read of "the people of the prince who is to come" who will destroy the city and the sanctuary. This corresponds remarkably with the unprecedented destruction wrought upon Jerusalem by the Roman legions of Titus in 70 C.E.

Even if one were to totally *avoid* the startling evidence of those computations, one fact stands crystal-clear in this passage—the Messiah had to come *before* the destruction of the Temple and of the holy city. If Jesus is not the Messiah, what figure in His generation was?

Does Daniel's prophecy point to Jesus? Decide for yourself.

8
Benedict Arnold Goes to a Seder

During His three years of public activity, Jesus repeatedly told His disciples that He would be betrayed into the hands of men and be executed.[1] In a portion of the New Testament that reads almost like a modern mystery, the agent of this betrayal turns out to be one of His twelve closest disciples, a man named Judas Iscariot. Here's how it happened.

After He arrived in Jerusalem, Jesus arranged to eat his last meal, a Passover Seder, with the twelve. That was on Thursday evening prior to His execution the next afternoon. As they went through the ancient rite, He spoke of the fulfillment of the ninth verse of Psalm 41, "He who eats My bread has lifted his heel against Me" (John 13:18).

Later, when they were still gathered around the table together, in an ironic counterpoint to the Passover themes of freedom and redemption, Jesus announced more clearly, "One of you will betray Me" (John 13:21). That this was said at a Seder stirred the disciples' curiosity all the more. They urged John, who reclined closest to Jesus, to ask whom He meant. When he did, Jesus replied, "That is the

---

1. Mark 9:31.

41

one for whom I shall dip the morsel and give it to him"
(John 13:26).

It was, and still is in the Middle East, a token of intimacy
to allow a guest to dip his bread in the common dish. Thus
Jesus reaffirmed His closeness to Judas as He handed him
the "morsel," which may have been the *karpas* or perhaps
the *charoses*. Then Judas slipped into the night to perform
his treachery. Precisely what information he delivered to
the religious authorities may never be known. Perhaps he
simply divulged the location of Jesus' overnight place of
prayer in Gethsemane. Certainly with that information the
authorities could arrest Jesus quietly without stirring up the
crowds that often applauded and supported Him.

Matthew details the transaction for us. He reports that
Judas had gone to the authorities before this final Seder to
ask what they would pay him to betray Jesus. The price
they offered: thirty pieces of silver, the price of a common
slave. Without blinking an eye, Judas accepted. But later,
when he saw that his betrayal would cost Jesus his life, he
was seized with horror and fear and tried to return the
money to the priests, "for I have betrayed innocent blood."
But the priests, aware of the seriousness of the situation,
were in no mood for refunds. So Judas threw the money
down in the Temple, left, and committed suicide. The
priests used the money to purchase a potter's field in which
to bury strangers. Some 500 years before this, Zechariah
had symbolically acted out this very scene, with himself in
the role of a good shepherd, a title Jesus used of Himself,
and the value placed on him as thirty pieces of silver.
Jeremiah also speaks of purchasing a field. Collections of
related prophetic messages seem to have existed, listed by
the name of one of the prophets. Matthew thus refers to

these two passages by combining them in a traditional manner under one heading, "Jeremiah" (see Matthew 27:3-10; Zechariah 11:12-13; Jeremiah 32:6-15).

The actual betrayal probably took place after midnight on the night of the Last Supper.* Judas led soldiers of the Temple guard and a party of others to Jesus' nocturnal retreat and identified Him to them by greeting Him with a kiss. As if to emphasize the enormity of this betrayal of trust, Jesus gives almost cosmic significance to the moment:

> And Jesus said to the chief priests and officers of the temple and elders who had come against Him, "Have you come out with swords and clubs as against a robber? While I was with you daily in the temple, you did not lay hands on Me; but this hour and the power of darkness are yours" [Luke 22:52-53].

Thus began a sequence of trials and mistreatment that continued through the rest of the early predawn hours and into the morning, till Pilate* at last consented to the cries of the mob and ordered the execution of Jesus. That was not the end of the story, however. An uncanny series of details followed. Events occurred that had been prescribed for this day hundreds of years before in the Scriptures—not the sort of things that would have stood out to readers before the events of Jesus' crucifixion, nor the sort of things that any but the most sensitive of observers would have noticed. As those fulfilled prophetic details come to a reader's attention, one feels a profound sense of awe and mystery—a feeling that things unseen may well be more powerful and real than things seen. Let us next examine some of those extraordinary details.

9
The Crucifixion Psalm

"My God, my God, why hast thou forsaken me?" was one of the few things Jesus uttered as He endured the agony of crucifixion. They were not words He dreamed up, but the words of His forefather David, the opening line of the twenty-second psalm. Other verses of that same psalm hold a special interest for us:

> But I am a worm, and no man; a reproach of men, and despised of the people. All they that see me laugh me to scorn; they shoot out the lip, they shake the head: "Let him commit himself unto the Lord! let Him rescue him; let Him deliver him, seeing He delighteth in him" [Psalm 22:7-9].

A comparison with the gospel accounts of the crucifixion would reveal some striking similarities:

> And even the rulers were sneering at Him, saying, "He saved others; let Him save Himself if this is the Christ of God, His Chosen One" [Luke 23:35].

> And those passing by were hurling abuse at Him, wagging their heads, and saying, "Ha! You who are going to destroy the temple and rebuild it in three days, save Yourself and come down from the cross!" In the same way the chief priests also, along with the scribes, were mocking Him among themselves . . . And those who were crucified with Him were casting the same insult at Him [Mark 15:29-32].

Later in the psalm of David we read:

I am poured out like water, and all my bones are out of joint; my heart is become like wax; it is melted in mine inmost parts. My strength is dried up like a potsherd; and my tongue cleaveth to my throat; and Thou layest me in the dust of death [Psalm 22:15-16].

As poetry, those lines are highly effective in their emotional impact. But beyond being mere poetic description, they are, as physicians have commented, surprisingly clinical descriptions of the sufferings of those undergoing crucifixion!

The next stanza continues:

For dogs have compassed me: the assembly of the wicked have enclosed me: they pierced my hands and my feet. I may tell all my bones: they look and stare upon me. They part my garments and cast lots upon my vesture [Psalm 22:17-19, Harkavy translation].

The reference to pierced hands and feet is quite peculiar since that practice did not characterize any form of punishment prescribed in the Torah or practiced in ancient Israel or any surrounding nations of the time. Only the later Roman savagery of nailing a man to a cross comes to mind as one reads David's words here. However, some of the words themselves are in dispute. The early Greek, Syriac, and Latin translations of the Scriptures all read it as we have it above. The Masoretic* text of the Hebrew, on the other hand, prefers "like a lion" in place of "they have pierced." This produces the unlikely reading, "like a lion my hands and feet" which is construed to mean "like a lion they were at my hands and feet." We can probably best understand what happened when we realize that, in

45

Hebrew, the phrase "they have pierced" is *kaaru* while "like a lion" is *kaari*. The words are identical except that "pierced" ends with the Hebrew letter *vav* and "lion" with *yod*. *Vav* and *yod* are similar in form, and a scribe might easily have changed the text by inscribing a *yod* and failing to attach a vertical descending line so that it would become a *vav*. The evidence suggests that this may be what happened, since the Greek version of the Scriptures, rendered in Egypt before the time of Jesus, preserves the reading of "pierced."

However, the fact that people cast lots for his clothing is clear and undisputed in the text of Psalm 22. Nor does anyone dispute that the detachment of Roman soldiers who carried out Jesus' execution did precisely that:

> The soldiers therefore, when they had crucified Jesus, took His outer garments and made four parts, a part to every soldier and also the tunic; now the tunic was seamless, woven in one piece. They said therefore to one another, "Let us not tear it, but cast lots for it, to decide whose it shall be" [John 19:23-24].

There is nothing contrived and nothing deliberate in this. The uncanniness of it all is disconcerting to those who don't know that behind the scenes there is a God who "declares unto us the things that shall happen . . . and announces to us things to come" (Isaiah 41:22).

10
An Unrefreshing Drink

After this, Jesus, knowing that all things had already been accomplished, in order that the Scripture might be fulfilled, said, "I am thirsty." A jar full of sour wine was standing there; so they put a sponge full of the sour wine upon a branch of hyssop, and brought it up to His mouth. When Jesus therefore had received the sour wine, He said, "It is finished!" And He bowed His head, and gave up His spirit [John 19:28-30].

What did John mean by saying that Jesus was doing this to fulfill the Scripture? Was Jesus so in control even in His final agony that He was busily trying to make sure He fulfilled all the prophecies pertaining to this event before He died, something like checking off a shopping list? Perhaps, but it seems more likely that He really was thirsty and cried out these words for that reason! By the words "that the Scripture might be fulfilled," John is showing us that the fulfillment of prophecy is evidence of God's hand at work in history.

But to what Scripture was John referring? Only one candidate presents itself:

Thou knowest my reproach, and my shame and my confusion; mine adversaries are all before Thee. Reproach hath broken my heart; and I am sore sick; and I looked for some to show compassion, but there was none; and for comforters, but I found none. Yea, they put poison into my food; and in my thirst they gave me vinegar to drink [Psalm 69:20-22].

Again, the parallel is too exact to simply be a coincidence—especially when you consider that the psalm was written some one thousand years before Jesus was even born.

11
Bones, Bones, Bones

The crucifixion of Jesus most likely took place on the eve of Passover, along with that of two thieves. The religious authorities asked Pilate to have the legs of all three broken in order to hasten their deaths and prevent their bodies from remaining displayed during the holiday. What they requested was for purely religious reasons; we might call it a "mercy killing." In order to appreciate what it was they were requesting, we need to have a little physiology lesson. Victims of crucifixion normally died slowly and painfully from asphyxiation, as they grew too weak to push up with their legs, thus allowing their lungs to function normally. Gradually, their lungs filled with carbon dioxide and they died. So you can see that breaking their legs would hasten their demise considerably.

> The soldiers therefore came, and broke the legs of the first man, and of the other man who was crucified with Him; but coming to Jesus, when they saw that He was already dead, they did not break His legs [John 19:32-33].

Jesus had once said that no one would take His life from Him, but that He would lay it down by His own choice.[1] Some men were actually known to have endured for days

---

1. John 10:18.

before dying on the cross. But Jesus did as He had said. He gave up His spirit, thereby avoiding broken bones and fulfilling His prophecy.

One of the major ideas in the New Testament is that Jesus is portrayed as a Passover lamb, and His life is seen as a counterpart to the story in Exodus where a perfect lamb is killed to provide redemption for the Israelites. That is why John especially notes the fulfillment of the regulation regarding the Passover lamb, that not a bone of it shall be broken.[2]

John continues,

> But one of the soldiers pierced His side with a spear, and immediately there came out blood and water. And he who has seen has borne witness, and his witness is true; and he knows that he is telling the truth, so that you also may believe. For these things came to pass, that the Scripture might be fulfilled . . . "THEY SHALL LOOK ON HIM WHOM THEY PIERCED" [John 19:34-37].

Remember the discussion of the pierced hands and feet in the last chapter? That was regarding Psalm 22, but there is another passage from Zechariah that also mentions piercing. This is the passage that John quoted above:

> And I will pour upon the house of David, and upon the inhabitants of Jerusalem, the spirit of grace and of supplication; and they shall look unto Me because they have thrust him through, and they shall mourn for him, as one mourneth for his only son, and shall be in bitterness for him, as one that is in bitterness for his first-born [Zechariah 12:10].

Jesus endured two sorts of piercing at his execution, and Psalm 22 and Zechariah 12:10 refer to them. Psalm 22 pic-

---

2. Exodus 12:46; John 19:36.

tured the piercing from the nails driven into the hands and feet. But when John quoted the Zechariah passage, he mentioned the spear that was driven into Jesus' side.

It is hard to be certain of the intent of John's comments about the blood and water. Modern physiology teaches us that blood in a cadaver readily separates into clear serum and red blood cells, thus certifying that the person is clinically dead. John could not possibly have known this; it is for him simply an eyewitness' detail, but it serves as a fulfillment of the prophecy.

Getting back to Zechariah, the entire twelfth chapter is an oracle about a day when Israel will be so strategically placed in world affairs that "all the nations of the earth shall be gathered together against it" (Zechariah 12:3). However, Zechariah continues, the Lord will so reinforce the house of David and Jerusalem that "he that stumbleth among them at that day shall be as David; and the house of David shall be as a godlike being, as the angel of the Lord before them. And it shall come to pass in that day, that I will seek to destroy all the nations that come against Jerusalem" (Zechariah 12:8-9).

Then according to verse 10, the inhabitants of Jerusalem will recognize the one whom they had pierced. That implies some former mistreatment of one who now is vindicated as righteous, just, and true, and who returns to rescue Israel out of a predicament even greater than that which she faced at the Red Sea. If this personage is indeed the Messiah, then He must have been present earlier in a different role in which He suffered and was pierced. Consequently, when the inhabitants of Jerusalem finally recognize Him and their mistake, they will repent with uncontrollable sorrow. A piece of apocalyptic* literature, written by a Jewish

Christian, accords with this: "BEHOLD, HE IS COMING WITH THE CLOUDS, and every eye will see Him, even those who pierced Him; and all the tribes of the earth will mourn over Him. Even so. Amen" (Revelation 1:7).

12
Resurrection!

Few people could live in the Western world today and be unaware of the Christian belief that Jesus rose from the dead. What is amazing, though, is that people will often reject that belief out of hand without ever examining the evidence to see whether it is true. In this chapter, we'll present some of that evidence.

The story is told of a young man who was pondering his dissatisfaction with the great religions of the world. He inquired of an old man as to what would prevent him from founding a new religion of his own, one more to his liking. The ancient reflected, "Not much, but it would be helpful if you could arrange to be executed and to rise from the dead on the third day."

There is unique importance to the death and resurrection of Jesus. The resurrection of Jesus was the great proclamation of the early church. So often did Paul link Jesus with the resurrection in his teaching, that when he went to Athens to preach the Christian message, the inhabitants, polytheistic Greeks that they were, misunderstood and thought that he was introducing them to two new gods, Jesus and Anastasis (*anastasis* being Greek for "resurrection")—gods that they could now merrily add to their pantheon!

The gospels devote large portions to the resurrection, describing how the disciples discovered Jesus' tomb to be empty three days after His burial; how they claimed to have seen Him alive, to have spoken with Him, to have dined with Him, to have touched His body and to have seen the marks of the wounds He had received in crucifixion; how they watched Him depart into heaven, and how, after the Holy Spirit came to dwell in them on Shavuot,* they began spreading the news with irrepressible enthusiasm.

Professor Ellis Rivkin of the Hebrew Union College Jewish Institute of Religion points out that the doctrine of the resurrection of the dead and the life of the world to come came to have new emphasis through the teaching of the Pharisees. Although the concept is found as far back as the books of Job (19:26-27) and Daniel (12:1-2), the problem posed by Roman persecution and domination led the Pharisees to expound and develop the idea further. Thus the Pharisees paved the way for the pivotal announcement of the early church that Jesus had risen from the dead, so confirming His claim to be the Messiah.

The Sadducees, the rationalists of their day and ideological opponents of the Pharisees, sought to entrap Jesus on the matter of the resurrection and consequently to embarrass the Pharisees. They proposed a situation in which one woman had been the wife of seven brothers in turn, as each brother died one after the other. "So in the resurrection," they asked, "whose wife will she be?"

> Jesus said to them, "Is this not the reason you are mistaken, that you do not understand the Scriptures, or the power of God? For when they rise from the dead, they neither marry, nor are given in marriage, but are like angels in heaven. But regarding the fact that the dead rise again, have you not read in the book of Moses, in the passage about the burning bush,

how God spoke to him, saying, 'I AM THE GOD OF ABRA-
HAM, AND THE GOD OF ISAAC, AND THE GOD OF JACOB'?
He is not the God of the dead, but of the living; you are
greatly mistaken" [Mark 12:24-27].

In this episode Jesus was fully on the side of the Pharisees. And, when Jesus' followers later declared that He had
risen from the dead, the Pharisees could not dismiss the
idea out of hand.

Peter first announced Jesus' resurrection publicly in
Jerusalem on Shavuot. In doing so he cited the sixteenth
psalm, in which David rejoiced because he believed God
would "not abandon my soul to the nether-world; neither
wilt Thou suffer Thy godly one to see the pit" (Psalm
16:10). Peter continues, "Brethren, I may confidently say
to you regarding the patriarch David that he both died and
was buried, and his tomb is with us to this day. And so,
because he was a prophet, and knew that GOD HAD SWORN
TO HIM WITH AN OATH TO SEAT one OF HIS DESCENDANTS
UPON HIS THRONE, he looked ahead and spoke of the resurrection of the Christ" [Acts 2:29-31].

Neither Jesus nor His disciples ever went further than
this to substantiate the resurrection from Scripture. They
didn't resort to Job or Daniel; they didn't need to. The idea
was ridiculous only to a few Sadducees. The bulk of the
people, influenced as they were by Pharisaical teaching,
found the claim reasonable and credible, something they at
least ought to investigate further.

And indeed, on further investigation the resurrection is
seen to be true. Run down the possibilities for yourself and
see which makes the best sense. Did the Roman authorities
steal the body of Jesus from the tomb? Then why didn't
they produce it when the word started being spread that

Jesus was risen? Or maybe the disciples stole it. But could such a fabrication on their part account for the change in their attitude? Three days earlier they were disillusioned idealists who had hoped that Jesus would change things around; could a lie now account for their hope, their boldness in the face of official persecution, and the high ethical standards they set? Perhaps Jesus never died; He just fainted on the cross and revived in the tomb. This idea was popularized in the book *The Passover Plot* some years back. Unfortunately the author overlooked the fact that the Romans pierced Jesus' side, making sure He was dead; also, there was a contingent of Roman guards watching the tomb as well as a huge stone that blocked its entrance. There was no way that a resuscitated Jesus could have escaped. Or was it all a hallucination? He must have been quite a hallucination to be seen by vastly different kinds of people at different times of day in many different places. You might be able to fool one person, but can you fool 500 who saw Him at one time? All things considered, maybe someone will excuse us if we believe that Jesus rose from the dead after all, just as He said! It certainly makes the most sense of the evidence. And it also explains the prophecy we've already talked about (chapter 3) in 2 Samuel 7, where one of David's descendants will reign forever. Presumably only one who has already died and now lives forever can possibly reign forever. Jesus seems once again to be the most likely candidate for that role.

13
The Suffering Servant

Can you imagine some giant, international megacorporation deciding that it was going to do something about the problems in the world and advertising for applicants for the position of Messiah? Probably in their résumés most of the applicants would emphasize their diplomatic skills, their prowess in waging war and bargaining for peace, and certainly the high reputation they had earned in other circles. Yet if the corporation knew its business, it would accept none of those applicants. Its executives would know that about 2,600 years ago, Isaiah already gave us a résumé for the Messiah, and that only one person in history ever matched those credentials.

This Messianic "résumé" occurs in four passages in Isaiah that scholars call the "Servant Songs." These songs are really four little vignettes. We encounter the first one in Isaiah 42:1-7. There we meet an unassuming character called the Servant of the Lord, whom God has endowed with His Spirit to bring justice to the nations. This Servant will work quietly and unobtrusively, yet without failure or discouragement, until He accomplishes His appointed task of bringing justice to the earth. No flashy shuttle diplomacy here!

Then, in Isaiah 49:1-6, we find the Servant addressing an audience of foreign nations and reporting a conversation between Himself and God. He tells them how the Lord called Him from birth, hand-crafted him, and kept Him in readiness for His mission, which is to restore Israel to God. And though He seems to feel that He has labored in vain, God intends Him to convey His salvation not only to Israel, but also to the Gentile nations.

The servant speaks again in Isaiah 50:4-9. He relates how God wakens Him daily so that He can listen to God. He has not turned back from His task, which He heard of when the Lord wakened Him. Instead, He hammered away at His work, even though it involved physical abuse. Nevertheless, His vindicator is near. He is confident that no one will be able to have Him arraigned and found guilty of anything.

Finally, though, we come to the centerpiece of messianic prophecy: Isaiah 52:13–53:12. Whereas the other three "Servant Songs" can refer to the responsibilities of the nation of Israel as well as to the Messiah, this passage unmistakably is speaking about a single individual. We'll look at this portion in detail, but first it will be helpful to get an overview of what people have thought of this chapter down through the centuries.

"OF WHOM DOES THE PROPHET SPEAK?"

Many throughout history have asked whom Isaiah is referring to, including an Ethiopian official who asked an early Jewish Christian named Philip.[1] Philip did not hesitate to identify the Servant of the Lord as Jesus. In fact, Jesus applied Isaiah 53 to Himself, quoting from it in Luke

---

1. Acts 8:30-35.

22:37 and alluding to one of its verses in Mark 10:45. But not everyone has been happy with the idea of a Messiah who suffers and dies.

The Servant Songs were regarded as messianic in Jewish writings from the beginning of the Common Era. However, since suffering and death were not exactly what people wanted in their Messiah, they regularly qualified their interpretation. For example, in a Targum of Isaiah—an Aramaic paraphrase of this same period—the phrases describing triumph are interpreted of the Messiah, but the Servant's sufferings are said to be descriptive of Israel and in some measure of the Gentiles too (see Appendix 1 for interpretations of this fourth Servant Song). Unfortunately, there is no warrant in the text for referring different parts of the prophecy to two different people or groups.

Later, as the Christians continued to press the messianic interpretation, most Jews, beginning in the Middle Ages with the famous rabbi Rashi, adopted a collective hypothesis that the Servant was Israel. This collective interpretation rests in part on Isaiah 49:3 where the Servant is addressed as Israel. But since we read there that the Servant's mission is primarily Israel, it must refer to some individual who incorporates the nation of Israel as a king might be said to embody his people.

More recently, in the eighteenth century, scholars have argued that Isaiah had a particular king in mind, such as Hezekiah, Uzziah, Jehoiachin, Zerubbabel, or Cyrus. Others have suggested Isaiah himself, or Jeremiah, or Moses, or some unknown contemporary of the prophet.

But none of those theories has a wide following today. Isaiah did not paint a portrait of one of his contemporaries in the Servant Songs. If the Servant begins as Israel, the picture becomes progressively individualized until in chapter 53, some one person is intended. Let's now turn to the passage itself and examine the ways in which the New Testament speaks of its fulfillment.

ECHOES OF THE KING-ON-A-DONKEY

Behold, My servant shall prosper, he shall be exalted and lifted up, and shall be very high. According as many were appalled at thee—so marred was his visage unlike that of a man, and his form unlike that of the sons of men—so shall he startle many nations, kings shall shut their mouths because of him; for that which had not been told them shall they see, and that which they had not heard shall they perceive [Isaiah 52:13-15].

The opening verses of the passage set the tone for the rest of the prophecy, and remind us of the same paradox we saw in Zechariah. There, you'll remember, we met the "King-on-a-donkey" who came in both great triumph and extreme humility. Here the same idea is repeated, and the following verses develop it in more detail.

THE UNPOPULAR KING

Who would have believed our report? And to whom hath the arm of the LORD been revealed? For he shot up right forth as a sapling, and as a root out of a dry ground; he had no form nor comeliness, that we should look upon him, nor beauty that we should delight in him. He was despised, and forsaken of men, a man of pains, and acquainted with disease, and as one from whom men hide their face: he was despised, and we esteemed him not" [Isaiah 53:1-3].

You do not need to be aware of the meticulous details of Jesus' life to see how those words might apply to Him. Have you ever seen those Hollywood movies of Jesus' life where Jesus stands on Pilate's balcony and hears the whole crowd crying out for His crucifixion? The production may be hokey, and Jesus may look more Danish than Jewish, but the scene is quite close to what actually happened. In a word, Jesus was rejected.

And His "visage," or face, was indeed marred so that He was left without any form or comeliness. The lashes of the Roman whip had disastrous consequences on a human body, and Jesus was subjected to hard, bruising blows about the face and head, and crowned with thorns. A look at John 19:1-3 will show how graphically this prophecy was fulfilled:

> Then Pilate therefore took Jesus, and scourged Him. And the soldiers wove a crown of thorns and put it on His head, and arrayed Him in a purple robe; and they began to come up to Him, and say, "Hail, King of the Jews!" and to give Him blows in the face.

An Unusual Remedy

The next words of the prophet describe how He took on Himself our griefs and sorrows (it could also mean sicknesses and pains in Hebrew), and how through His suffering, people could experience forgiveness for their sins:

> Surely our diseases he did bear, and our pains he carried; whereas we did esteem him stricken, smitten of God, and afflicted. But he was wounded because of our transgressions, he was crushed because of our iniquities; the chastisement of our welfare was upon him, and with his stripes we were

61

healed. All we like sheep did go astray, we turned everyone to his own way; and the LORD hath made to light on him the iniquity of us all [Isaiah 53:4-6].

Matthew explains in his gospel that when the townspeople of Capernaum brought to Him "many who were demon-possessed," Jesus cast out the spirits with a word and healed all who were sick. This, says Matthew, was "in order that what was spoken through Isaiah the prophet might be fulfilled, saying, 'HE HIMSELF TOOK OUR INFIRMITIES AND CARRIED AWAY OUR DISEASES'" (Matthew 8:16-17).

The second idea in this passage might seem strange to our twentieth-century minds: the idea that someone can suffer and die so that others might be spared. But it is not strange to the Bible. The entire system of animal sacrifices was based on this idea. It shows up again in the story in Genesis, where God provides a ram to die in Isaac's place just as Abraham is about to drive a knife into his heart.

It surfaces yet again in the New Testament, when John the Baptist, seeing Jesus coming toward him, announces, "Behold, the Lamb of God who takes away the sin of the world!" (John 1:29). Jesus, foreseeing His own death, spoke of giving His life as a ransom, or substitute, for many (Mark 10:45). From the very outset, the apostles offered their listeners forgiveness of sins in Jesus' name;[2] and their audience knew that such forgiveness was inextricably bound up with the idea of the sacrificial death of a substitute. Indeed, the references to the atoning nature of Jesus'

---

2. Acts 2:38.

suffering and death in the New Testament are too numerous to mention.

AN OPPRESSED SHEEP

Isaiah twice goes on to say that the Lord's servant was silent in the face of those who afflicted him. We read in Matthew that "And while He was being accused by the chief priests and elders, He made no answer. Then Pilate said to Him, 'Do you not hear how many things they testify against You?' And He did not answer him with regard to even a single charge, so that the governor was quite amazed" (Matthew 27:12-14). It is not that Jesus remained utterly mute throughout the time of His trial and execution; He did make a few remarks. There was however, no plea for mercy, no answer to the charges. His behavior could not have been more aptly characterized than by Isaiah's words:

> He was oppressed, though he humbled himself and he opened not his mouth; as a lamb that is led to the slaughter, and as a sheep that before her shearers is dumb; yea, he opened not his mouth [Isaiah 53:7].

The next verse reemphasizes most of what has already been said:

> By oppression and judgment he was taken away, and with his generation who did reason? For he was cut off out of the land of the living, for the transgression of my people to whom the stroke was due [Isaiah 53:8].

We then come to the strange mention of the Servant's grave:

> And they made his grave with the wicked, and with the rich in his tomb; although he had done no violence, neither was any deceit in his mouth [Isaiah 53:9].

It is not difficult to imagine a wealthy wicked man; history is full of them. But that is not how this prophecy was fulfilled for Jesus. He was buried in the tomb of Joseph of Arimathea, a wealthy but not unrighteous man.[3] Joseph was a member of the Sanhedrin and a respected Jewish leader. But Jesus had died a felon's death—crucifixion, the common way to punish criminals. Consequently, his grave would be considered a wicked man's grave. The words of Paul, a Jewish believer who had belonged to the party of the Pharisees, come to mind: "He [God] made Him [Jesus] who knew no sin to be sin on our behalf, that we might become the righteousness of God in Him" (2 Corinthians 5:21).

RESURRECTION REVISITED!

The next verse not only mentions that the Servant's death will be a sacrifice for sin, using the technical Hebrew term for this, *asham;* but it goes on to describe the life of the Servant after His death—in other words, His resurrection:

> Yet it pleased the LORD to crush him by disease; to see if his

---

3. Luke 23:50-53.

soul would offer itself in restitution [*asham*], that he might see his seed, prolong his days, and that the purpose of the LORD might prosper by his hand [Isaiah 53:10].

FINALE

The conclusion of Isaiah 53 mentions no new themes. Instead it reviews and underscores the dominant themes of the preceding verses. The Servant's death is really an act of God; when the Servant submits to it, much good comes of it, and He ends up sharing a place with the great.

Of the travail of his soul he shall see to the full, even My servant, who by his knowledge did justify the Righteous One to the many, and their iniquities he did bear. Therefore will I divide him a portion among the great, and he shall divide the spoil with the mighty; because he bared his soul unto death, and was numbered with the transgressors; yet he bore the sin of many, and made intercession for the transgressors [Isaiah 53:11-12].

"Of whom does the prophet speak?" The conclusion seems inescapable.

Postscript

I was extraordinarily naive when, as a relatively young man in the midst of my Jewish community in Denver, Colorado, I came to believe in Jesus. I actually believed that other Jews didn't believe simply because I hadn't told them, so I set out to tell them all. It didn't dawn on me for a long time that I had taken a "fool's" credentials when I took the name of Jesus. By becoming a friend of Jesus I became an "enemy" to those who disagreed or felt threatened by my newfound faith. In their eyes I became someone to be maligned. There wasn't much on me in the way of gossip, so they had to dig back in their memories to recall that I had once flunked Spanish, a sure sign of mental retardation. And then, too, there was the time I was laid off from a temporary sales clerk's job after the Christmas holidays. That got turned into a firing for who-knew-what dark reason.

I finally emerged from that season licking my wounds, older and, hopefully, wiser. One thing in particular began to dawn on me. My Jewish brethren were not the least bit interested in hearing my account of how I came to believe. Those circumstances that had had a profound bearing on my own life of faith were irrelevant to others. There had to be some other way. This is the way of which the apostle Peter spoke after he recounted the elements of his own eye-witness account. Though he even speaks of his presence with Jesus on the Mount of Transfiguration as evidence of the truth of what he says, he adds, "We have also a more sure word of prophecy" (2 Peter 1:19, KJV).†Better than an account of an eyewitness is the testimony of the Bible. When I recognized that, it changed the course of my career. Thereafter, when I went to my people with the message that Jesus was the Messiah, I did not offer only the evidence of my own changed life. Instead I offered the evidence of what my people revere as holy, the Law and the Prophets.

This was brought home to me in 1971 when I was speaking in a church. Afterward a man came up to me. "You probably don't remember me," he began after he introduced himself, "but eleven years ago you visited my home and talked to me about Christianity. I ridiculed you and your message. I blasphemed and I ordered you out of the house.

"I was so pleased with the way in which I felt I had utterly defeated you, that I decided to go to work on my neighbor, Irving Schwartz,[1] a man you had already won to your faith. So, I went to my rabbi to get him to show me how to refute your arguments from Isaiah 53. I had studied it pretty closely and decided I probably needed a little professional help.

"The rabbi said the suffering Servant was Israel. But I couldn't see how the pronouns lined up to justify that interpretation. I told the rabbi so, and he backed off with the suggestion that maybe Isaiah had Hezekiah in mind. His arguments seemed so weak, I decided to go elsewhere.

"The next expert told me that Isaiah 53 had never been

---

† King James Version.
1. Irving Schwartz is a pseudonym.

regarded by any Jews as a messianic text. Then, however, I came across the Targum of Jonathan, and I saw that there, at least, the passage was regarded as messianic.

"Well, when I saw that, I really began to wonder—and to pray. Finally, in 1966, I received Christ as my own Savior and Lord. Today I'm a deacon in this church."

Stories like that have sealed my understanding. We do have a more sure word of prophecy, vouched for both by Tanach* and the New Testament:

> I am the LORD, that is My name; and My glory will I not give to another, neither My praise to graven images. Behold, the former things are come to pass, and new things do I declare; before they spring forth I tell you of them [Isaiah 42:8-9].

> You do well to pay attention as to a lamp shining in a dark place, until the day dawns and the morning star arises in your hearts. But know this first of all, that no prophecy of Scripture is a matter of one's own interpretation, for no prophecy was ever made by an act of human will, but men moved by the Holy Spirit spoke from God [2 Peter 1:19-21].

May you, the reader of this book, be challenged and moved to consider these scriptural prophecies. They point to the fulfillment of the hopes and aspirations of our people in the person of Jesus of Nazareth, the Messiah of Israel.

APPENDIX 1
Biblical Passages Applied to the Messiah in Early Rabbinical Writings

The following rabbinical sources are given in the order the relevant biblical passages appear in the body of this book. The sources consulted and their approximate dates are as follows:

Targum Jonathan (early second century C.E.)

Targum Onkelos (second century C.E.)

Babylonian Talmud (final compilation, 500 C.E.)

Targum Yerushalmi (a fragmentary targum, perhaps sixth century C.E., but based on older sources)

Midrash Rabbah (various dates; the earliest [on Genesis] completed 600 C.E., and based on earlier sources)

Targum Pseudo-Jonathan (late seventh century C.E., but based on older sources)

Pesikta Rabbati (compilation ninth century C.E. at the latest, possibly much earlier; based on material dating back to Talmudic times)

Rashi (acronym for Rabbi Shlomo ben Yitzhak, who lived 1040–1105 C.E.)

Yalkut Shimoni (a work of the thirteenth century C.E.)

Ralbag (acronym for Rabbi Levi Ben Gershon, French rabbi, fourteenth century C.E.)

Micah 5:1

Targum Jonathan: And you, O Bethlehem Ephrath, you who were too small to be numbered among the thousands of the house of Judah, from you shall come forth before Me the Messiah, to exercise dominion over Israel, he whose name was mentioned from before, from the days of creation.[1]

Genesis 3:1

Targum Yerushalmi: And it shall be that when the sons of the woman study the Torah diligently and obey its injunctions, they will direct themselves to smite you on the head and slay you; but when the sons of the woman forsake the commandments of the Torah and do not obey its injunctions, you will direct yourself to bite them on the heel and afflict them. However, there will be a remedy for the sons of the woman, but for you, serpent, there will be no remedy. They shall make peace with one another in the end, in the very end of days, in the days of the King Messiah.[2]

Genesis 23:5

Midrash Rabbah: R. Tanhuma said in the name of Samuel Kozith: (She hinted at) that seed which would arise

---

1. Samson H. Levey, "Targums" in *The Messiah: An Aramaic Interpretation; The Messianic Exegesis of the Targum* (Cincinnati: Hebrew Union College Jewish Institute of Religion, 1974), p. 92.
2. Ibid., p. 2.

from another source, viz. the king Messiah. [This midrash deals with Eve's naming of Seth.][3]

Targum Pseudo-Jonathan. I will put enmity between you and the woman, and between the offspring of your sons and the offspring of her sons; and it shall be that when the sons of the woman observe the commandments of the Torah, they will direct themselves to smite you on the head, but when they forsake the commandments of the Torah you will direct yourself to bite them on the heel. However, there is a remedy for them, but no remedy for you. They are destined to make peace in the end, in the days of the King Messiah.[4]

Genesis 49:10

Targum Onkelos: The transmission of dominion shall not cease from the house of Judah, nor the scribe from his children's children, forever, until the Messiah comes, to whom the Kingdom belongs, and whom nations shall obey.[5]

Targum Pseudo-Jonathan: Kings and rulers shall not cease from the house of Judah, nor scribes who teach the Torah from his seed, until the time when the King Messiah shall come, the youngest of his sons, and because of him nations shall melt away.[6]

Targum Yerushalmi: Kings shall not cease from the house of Judah, nor scribes who teach the Torah from his children's children, until the time of the coming of the King

3. H. Freedman and Maurice Simon, eds., *Midrash Rabbah* (London: Soncino, 1939), p. 196.
4. Levey, p. 2.
5. *Ibid.*, p. 7.
6. *Ibid.*, p. 8.

Messiah, to whom belongs the Kingdom, and to whom all dominions of the earth shall become subservient.[7]

Sanhedrin 98b: R. Johanan said: [The world was created] For the sake of the Messiah. What is his (the Messiah's) name?—The School of R. Shila said: His name is Shiloh, for it is written: *Until Shiloh come.*[8]

Deut. 18:18

Ralbag (His comments here are based on an earlier midrash): *A prophet from the midst of thee.* In fact the Messiah is such a Prophet as it is stated in the Midrash [Tanhuma] on the verse *Behold my Servant shall prosper* [Isaiah 52:13] ... Moses by the miracles which he wrought brought a single nation to the worship of God, but the Messiah will draw all peoples to the worship of God.[9]

Zech. 9:9

Sanh. 98a [referring also to Daniel 7:13]: R. Alexandri said: R. Joshua opposed two verses: it is written, *And behold, one like the son of man came with the clouds of heaven*; whilst (elsewhere) it is written, *(behold, thy king cometh unto thee ...) lowly, and riding upon an ass!*—If they are meritorious, (he will come) *with the clouds of heaven;* if not, *lowly and riding upon an ass.*[10]

Ber. 56b: If one sees an ass in a dream, he may hope for salvation, as it says, *Behold thy king cometh unto thee; he is triumphant and victorious, lowly and riding upon an ass.*[11]

7. *Ibid.,* p. 11.
8. "Sanhedrin," Vol. 3 of *Nezikin,* Babylonian Talmud, edited by Isidore Epstein, reprint (London: Soncino, 1938), p. 668.
9. Rachmiel Frydland, *Messianic Prophecy* (unpublished manuscript, 1980).
10. *Nezikin,* vol. 3, Babylonian Talmud, pp. 663–64.
11. *Zeraim,* Babylonian Talmud, p. 350.

Possibly Daniel 9:24-27

Megillah 3a: The *Targum* of the Prophets was composed by Jonathan ben Uzziel under the guidance of Haggai, Zechariah and Malachi ... and a Bath Kol [voice from heaven] came forth and exclaimed, Who is this that has revealed My secrets to mankind? ... He further sought to reveal (by) a targum (the inner meaning) of the Hagiographa [portion of Scripture which includes Daniel], but a Bath Kol went forth and said, Enough! What was the reason?—Because the date of the Messiah is foretold in it.[12]

Zech. 12:10

Sukk. 52a: What is the cause of the mourning [of Zech. 12:12]— ... It is well according to him who explains that the cause is the slaying of Messiah the son of Joseph, since that well agrees with the Scriptural verse, *And they shall look upon me because they have thrust him through, and they shall mourn for him as one mourneth for his only son;* [Zech. 12:10] ... [13]

Raphael Patai remarks: "Scholars have repeatedly speculated about the origin of the Messiah ben Joseph legend and the curious fact that the Messiah figure has thus been split in two. It would seem that in the early legend, the death of the Messiah was envisaged, perhaps as a development of the Suffering Servant motif. ... When the death of the Messiah became an established tenet in Talmudic times, this was felt to be irreconcilable with the belief in the Messiah as the Redeemer who would usher in the blissful millennium of the Messianic age. The dilemma was solved by splitting the person of the Messiah in two: one of them,

---

12. "Megillah," vol. 4 of *Mo'ed*, Babylonian Talmud, p. 10.
13. "Sukkah," vol. 3 of *Mo'ed*, Babylonian Talmud, p. 246.

called Messiah ben Joseph, was to raise the armies of Israel against their enemies, and, after many victories and miracles, would fall victim to Gog and Magog. The other, Messiah ben David, will come after him (in some legends will bring him back to life, which psychologically hints at the identity of the two), and will lead Israel to the ultimate victory, the triumph, and the Messianic era of bliss."[14]

Psalm 22

Pesikta Rabbati, Piska 36:1-2: (At the time of the Messiah's creation), the Holy One, blessed be He, will tell him in detail what will befall him: There are souls that have been put away with thee under My throne, and it is their sins which will bend thee down under a yoke of iron and make thee like a calf whose eyes grow dim with suffering, ... During the seven-year period preceding the coming of the son of David, iron beams will be brought and loaded upon his neck until the Messiah's body is bent low... It was because of the ordeal of the son of David that David wept, saying, *My strength is dried up like a potsherd* (Ps.22:16).[15]

Yalkut Shimoni (687): *Many dogs have encompassed me*— this refers to Haman's sons. *The assembly of the wicked have enclosed me*—this refers to Ahasuerus and his crowd. *"Kaari" my hands and my feet*—Rabbi Nehemiah says, "They pierced my hands and my feet in the presence of Ahasuerus." [This shows that the reading "pierced" was accepted by certain rabbis.][16]

14. Raphael Patai, *The Messiah Texts* (New York: Avon, 1979), p. 166.
15. William G. Braude, trans. *Pesikta Rabbati* (New Haven, Conn.: Yale U., 1968), pp. 678–80.
16. Frydland.

Isaiah 52:13—53:12

Targum Jonathan: 52:13. Behold, My servant the Messiah shall prosper; he shall be exalted and great and very powerful.

v.14. As the house of Israel, their appearance darkened among the nations, and their bright countenance darkened among the children of men, looked for him many days.

v.15. So shall he scatter many nations. Kings shall be silent concerning him, they shall place their hands on their mouths, for that which had not been related to them they have seen, and that which they had not heard they will understand.

53:1. Who would have believed this, our good tidings, and the powerful arm of the might of the Lord, for whom is it now revealed?

v.2. The Righteous One shall grow up before Him, lo, like sprouting plants; and like a tree that sends its roots by the water-courses, so shall the exploits of the holy one multiply in the land which was desperate for him. His appearance shall not be a profane appearance, nor shall the awe of him be the awe of an ignorant person, but his countenance shall radiate with holiness, so that all who see him shall become wise through him.

v.3. Then he shall be contemptuous of, and bring to an end, the glory of all the kingdoms; they shall become weak and afflicted, lo, like a man in pain and accustomed to illness, and like us, when the Shekinah had departed from us, leaving us despised and without esteem.

v.4. Then he shall seek pardon for our sins, and our iniquities shall be forgiven for his sake; though we are considered stricken, smitten by God, and afflicted.

v.5. And he shall rebuild the Temple, which was profaned because of our sins, and which was surrendered because of our iniquities; through his instruction, his peace shall abound for us, and when we teach his words our sins shall be forgiven us.

v.6. All of us were scattered like sheep, we were exiled, each in his own direction, but it is the will of God to pardon the sins of all of us on his account.

v.7. He asked in prayer and was answered, and it was accepted even before he could open his mouth; he shall deliver the mighty of the nations like a lamb to the slaughter; and like a lamb that is silent before its shearers, there shall be none to open his mouth and say a word against him.

v.8. He shall gather in our exiles from their pain and punishment. Who shall be able to recount the wonders which shall be performed for us in his days, for he shall remove the domination of the nations from the land of Israel. And the sins which My people have committed, he shall account unto them.

v.9. And he shall deliver the wicked into Gehenna, and those rich in possessions which we had lost, taken by force at death; so that those who commit sin shall not prevail and shall not speak deceitful things with their mouth.

v.10. It is the will of the Lord to purify and to acquit as innocent the remnant of His people, to cleanse their souls of sin, so that they may see the kingdom of their Messiah, have many sons and daughters, enjoy long life, and observe the Torah of the Lord, prospering according to His will.

v.11. He shall save them from the servitude of the nations, they shall see the punishment of their enemies and be sated with the spoil of their kings. By his wisdom he shall vindicate the meritorious, in order to bring many to be subservient to the Torah, and he shall seek forgiveness for their sins.

v.12. Then I will apportion unto him the spoil of great nations, and he shall divide as spoil the wealth of mighty cities, because he was ready to suffer martyrdom that the rebellious he might subjugate to the Torah. And he shall seek pardon for the sins of many and for his sake the rebellious shall be forgiven.[17]

In addition, an older edition of the Machzor contains this in the Musaf (additional) Service for Yom Kippur:

> Our righteous anointed is departed from us: horror hath seized us, and we have none to justify us. He hath borne the yoke of our iniquities, and our transgression, and is wounded because of our transgression. He beareth our sins on his shoulder, that he may find pardon for our iniquities. We shall be healed by his wound, at the time that the Eternal will create him (the Messiah) as a new creature. O bring him up from the circle of the earth. Raise him up from Seir, to assemble us the second time on Mount Lebanon, by the hand of Yinon [one of the rabbinic names of the Messiah].[18]

17. Levey, pp. 63–66.
18. A. Th. Phillips, ed. *Machzor for Rosh Hashana and Yom Kippur*, rev. ed. (New York: Hebrew Publishing, 1931), p. 239.

APPENDIX 2
Mikveh and Baptism

CEREMONIAL WASHINGS IN BIBLICAL TIMES

All these water rituals formed the basis for the Jewish *mikveh* laws. Although the Hebrew word *mikveh* means literally "a collection" or "gathering together," in this context it refers to a gathering or pool of water for the purpose of ritual cleansing. The earliest biblical usage of the word *mikveh* occurs in Genesis 1:10, which describes the "gathered waters" which God then names "seas."

These washings were for the purpose of symbolic cleansing to demonstrate a spiritual purity:

Exodus 19:10. Even before the giving of the Torah at Sinai, God commanded the people to wash their clothing as a symbolic act of purification.

Leviticus 8:6. Aaron and his sons washed when they were ordained as priests to minister in the Tabernacle.

Leviticus 16:4. Again Aaron had to wash himself before and after (v. 24) he ministered in the Holy of Holies on Yom Kippur.

Numbers 19:7ff. There are explicit instructions for purification after defilement by a dead body. After bathing and washing his clothes, the "unclean" person had to be sprin-

kled with fresh water combined with ashes from a sacri-
ficed animal.

Numbers 31:21-24. The Israelites used the "water of
sprinkling" to purify themselves and their plunder after
they battled with the Midianites.

Leviticus 13-15. The Torah commanded ritual purification for both men and women who had been "defiled" by
flows of various bodily fluids, or who had been healed of
leprosy.

CEREMONIAL IMMERSION IN POST-BIBLICAL JUDAISM

Another use of symbolic purification by water became
part of early Jewish tradition. It was immersion, or *tevilah,*
for Gentile converts to Judaism. "Baptism" is the Greek-
derived equivalent of *tevilah* from the Greek verb *baptidzo;*
hence, we may speak of such converts as being immersed or
baptized.

Although the only biblical requirement for entrance into
the covenant was circumcision, baptism became an added
requisite. No one knows exactly when or by whom the
requirements were changed to include baptism, but it was
before the time of Jesus, as we learn from debates on the
subject of proselyte baptism between the rabbinic schools
of Shammai and Hillel, both contemporaries of Jesus.
Whereas the school of Shammai stressed circumcision as
the point of transition, the Hillelites considered baptism
most important because it portrayed spiritual cleansing and
the beginning of a new life. Ultimately the Hillelite view
prevailed, as reflected in the Talmudic writings. The

revered twelfth-century Jewish sage Maimonides summed up the Talmudic tradition concerning converts to Judaism:

> By three things did Israel enter into the Covenant: by circumcision and baptism and sacrifice. Circumcision was in Egypt, as it is written: *No uncircumcised person shall eat thereof* (Exodus 12:48). Baptism was in the wilderness just before the giving of the Law, as it is written: *Sanctify them today and tomorrow, and let them wash their clothes* (Exodus 19:10). And sacrifice, as it is said: *And he sent young men of the children of Israel which offered burnt offerings* (Exodus 24:5).... When a gentile is willing to enter the covenant ... he must be circumcised and be baptized and bring a sacrifice.... And at this time when there is no sacrifice, they must be circumcised and be baptized; and when the Temple shall be built, they are to bring a sacrifice.... The gentile that is made a proselyte and the slave that is made free, behold he is like a child new born.[1]

Presently a Gentile who would embrace Judaism must undergo baptism in a *mikveh* ritual. The purpose of this ceremonial immersion is to portray spiritual cleansing, as Maimonides concluded in his codification of the laws of *mikveh:*

> ... uncleanness is not mud or filth which water can remove, but it is a matter of scriptural decree and dependent on the intention of the heart.[2]

CEREMONIAL IMMERSION AND JOHN THE BAPTIST

The activity of Yochanan ben Zechariah, generally known to history as John the Baptist, is in line with cere-

1. Ceil Rosen, "Baptism—Pagan or Jewish?" *Issues* 2, 10 (1981) :3.
2. *Ibid.*

monial washings and immersions in Judaism. John's emphasis that repentance be visibly demonstrated by baptism was in keeping with the ritual use of water elsewhere to signify a spiritual renewal (see chapter 5).

CEREMONIAL IMMERSION AND THE NEW TESTAMENT

The New Testament ascribes a multiple symbolism to the baptism of believers in Jesus the Messiah.

Titus 3:5. Here baptism is depicted as the washing away of sin and uncleanness and the giving of new life by God's Spirit to those who are thus cleansed. This symbolism has its roots in the ideas already found in the Torah.

Romans 6:3-4. This further describes baptism as a picture of death and resurrection, a symbolism not found previously. That is, by his baptism the believer publicly announces that through faith in the Messiah, he has died to his old sinful ways and has been made alive to God. As in Jewish tradition, baptism followed the order whereby a candidate first assented to the beliefs he was to hold and then was immersed. Those who believe in the Messiah are plunged or buried into His atoning death, so that God might raise them to a new life as He raised the Messiah from the dead.

APPENDIX 3
Conversion in Tanach and the New Testament

The connotation of *conversion* to mean leaving one religion for another is completely foreign to the Scriptures. There rather, the idea is turning or returning to God, and the Hebrew term employed is *shuv*. Examples of its use will demonstrate this.

USED OF FOREIGN NATIONS

Jonah 3:10. And God saw their works, that they *turned* from their evil way; and God repented of the evil, which He said He would do unto them.

USED OF INDIVIDUALS' CONVERSIONS

Psalm 51:15. Then will I teach transgressors Thy ways, and sinners shall *return* unto Thee.

2 Kings 23:25. And like unto him was there no king before him, that *turned* to the LORD with all his heart, and with all his soul, and with all his might.

USED OF WORLD-WIDE CONVERSION

Psalm 22:28. All the ends of the earth shall remember and *turn* unto the LORD.

(The *return* of those who at one point had turned to God.)

Deuteronomy 4:30. In thy distress, when all these things are come upon thee, in the end of days, thou wilt *return* to the LORD thy God and hearken unto His voice.

Deuteronomy 30:2. [When thou] shalt *return* unto the LORD thy God, and hearken to His voice according to all that I command thee this day, thou and thy children, with all thy heart, and with all thy soul; that then the LORD thy God will turn thy captivity.

Zechariah 1:3. Therefore say thou unto them: Thus saith the LORD of hosts: *Return* unto Me, saith the LORD of hosts, and I will *return* unto you, saith the LORD of hosts.

Isaiah 6:9-10. Hear ye indeed, but understand not; and see ye indeed, but perceive not. Make the heart of this people fat, and make their ears heavy, and shut their eyes; lest they, seeing with their eyes, and hearing with their ears, and understanding with their heart, *return* and be healed.

Jeremiah 24:7. And I will give them a heart to know Me, that I am the LORD; and they shall be my people, and I will be their God; for they shall *return* unto Me with their whole heart.

(Used to show that conversion is God's doing as well as man's responsibility.)

Jeremiah 31:18. Turn thou me, and I shall be *turned*, for Thou art the LORD my God.

Lamentations 5:21. Turn Thou us unto Thee, O LORD, and we shall be *turned*.

IN THE NEW TESTAMENT

(Not a change of religion, or abandonment of heritage, but a turning to God.)

OF JEWS

Matthew 18:3. And he said, "I tell you the truth, unless you *change* [literally, *turn*] and become like little children, you will never enter the kingdom of heaven" (NIV).†

Acts 3:19. Repent, then, and *turn* to God, so that your sins may be wiped out, that times of refreshing may come from the Lord (NIV).

OF GENTILES

Acts 14:15. We are bringing you good news, telling you to *turn* from these worthless things to the living God, who made heaven and earth and sea and everything in them (NIV).

1 Thessalonians 1:9. They tell us how you *turned* to God from idols to serve the living and true God (NIV).

OF BOTH JEWS AND GENTILES

Acts 26:20. First to those in Damascus, then to those in Jerusalem and in all Judea, and to the Gentiles also, I preached that they should repent and *turn* to God and prove their repentance by their deeds (NIV).

1 Peter 2:25. For you were like sheep going astray, but now you have *returned* to the Shepherd and Overseer of your souls (NIV).

---

† *New International Version.*

APPENDIX 4
Israel and the Gentiles

Many portions of Scripture speak of the last days of history when the *goyim,* or Gentiles, will wage war against Israel. What is not as well known is that many verses of Scripture speak of God's blessings upon the Gentiles and even of their inclusion with Israel as part of God's people. It should not be surprising that the message of Jesus has been open to Gentiles as well as Jews, for that was God's plan from the very start. The following is a compilation of some of those passages.

GENTILES TO BE BLESSED THROUGH ISRAEL

Genesis 12:1-3. Now the LORD said unto Abram: "Get thee out of thy country, and from thy kindred, and from thy father's house, unto the land that I will show thee. And I will make of thee a great nation, and I will bless thee, and make thy name great; and be thou a blessing. And I will bless them that bless thee, and him that curseth thee will I curse; and in thee shall all the families of the earth be blessed."

Genesis 18:17-18. And the LORD said: "Shall I hide from Abraham that which I am doing; seeing that Abraham shall surely become a great and mighty nation, and all the nations of the earth shall be blessed in him?"

Genesis 26:3-4. "Sojourn in this land, and I will be with thee, and will bless thee; for unto thee, and unto thy seed, I will give all these lands, and I will establish the oath which I swore unto Abraham thy father; and I will multiply thy seed as the stars of heaven, and will give unto thy seed all these lands; and by thy seed shall all the nations of the earth bless themselves."

Genesis 28:13-14. And, behold, the LORD stood beside him, and said: "I am the LORD, the God of Abraham thy father, and the God of Isaac. The land whereon thou liest, to thee will I give it, and to thy seed. And thy seed shall be as the dust of the earth, and thou shalt spread abroad to the west, and to the east, and to the north, and to the south. And in thee and in thy seed shall all the families of the earth be blessed."

Psalm 72:17. [Said of King Solomon] May his name endure for ever; May his name be continued as long as the sun; May men also bless themselves by him; May all nations call him happy.

GOD TO BLESS THE GENTILES

2 Samuel 7:18-19. Then David the king went in, and sat before the LORD; and he said: "Who am I, O LORD God, and what is my house, that Thou hast brought me thus far? And this was yet a small thing in Thine eyes, O LORD God; but Thou hast spoken also of Thy servant's house for a great while to come; and this too after the manner of great men, O LORD God."

The phrase *torath ha-adam* is translated "after the manner of great men." An alternate translation is "and this is the 'Torah of Mankind,'" implying that all God has promised to David would affect not only the Jewish people, but all other nations as well.

Jeremiah 4:1-2. If thou wilt return, O Israel, saith the LORD, Yea, return unto Me; and if thou wilt put away thy detestable things out of My sight, and wilt not waver; and wilt swear: "As the LORD liveth" in truth, in justice, and in righteousness; then shall the nations bless themselves by Him, and in Him shall they glory.

ISRAEL AND HER MESSIAH TO BE SPIRITUAL LIGHTS TO THE GENTILES

Isaiah 11:10. And it shall come to pass in that day, that the root of Jesse, that standeth for an ensign of the peoples, unto him shall the nations seek; And his resting-place shall be glorious.

Isaiah 42:1, 4, 6. Behold My servant, whom I uphold; Mine elect, in whom My soul delighteth; I have put My spirit upon him, He shall make the right to go forth to the nations.

He shall not fail nor be crushed, till he have set the right in the earth; and the isles shall wait for his teaching.

I the LORD have called thee in righteousness, and have taken hold of thy hand, and kept thee, and set thee for a covenant of the people, for a light of the nations.

Isaiah 49:6. Yea, He saith: "It is too light a thing that thou shouldest be My servant To raise up the tribes of Jacob, and to restore the offspring of Israel; I will also give thee for a light of the nations, that My salvation may be unto the end of the earth."

God to Treat the Gentiles as Equals with Israel

Isaiah 19:19-25. In that day shall there be an altar to the LORD in the midst of the land of Egypt, and a pillar at the border thereof to the LORD. And it shall be for a sign and for a witness unto the LORD of hosts in the land of Egypt; for they shall cry unto the LORD because of the oppressors, and He will send them a saviour, and a defender, who will deliver them. And the LORD shall make Himself known to Egypt, and the Egyptians shall know the LORD in that day; yea, they shall worship with sacrifice and offering, and shall vow a vow unto the LORD, and shall perform it. And the LORD will smite Egypt, smiting and healing; and they shall return unto the LORD, and He will be entreated of them, and will heal them. In that day shall there be a highway out of Egypt to Assyria, and the Assyrian shall come into Egypt, and the Egyptian into Assyria; and the Egyptians shall worship with the Assyrians. In that day shall Israel be the third with Egypt and with Assyria, a blessing in the midst of the earth; for that the LORD of hosts hath blessed him, saying: "Blessed be Egypt My people and Assyria the work of My hands, and Israel Mine inheritance."

Joel 3:1, 5. And it shall come to pass afterward, that I will pour out My spirit upon all flesh.

And it shall come to pass, that whosoever shall call on the name of the LORD shall be delivered.

Amos 9:11-12. In that day will I raise up the tabernacle of David that is fallen, and close up the breaches thereof, and I will raise up his ruins, and I will build it as in the days of old; that they may possess the remnant of Edom, and all the nations, upon whom My name is called, saith the LORD that doeth this.

Zechariah 2:14-15. "Sing and rejoice, O daughter of Zion; for, lo, I come, and I will dwell in the midst of thee, saith the LORD. And many nations shall join themselves to the LORD in that day, and shall be My people, and I will dwell in the midst of thee."

THE GENTILES TO PRAY TO, WORSHIP, AND KNOW THE GOD OF ISRAEL

1 Kings 8:41-43, 59-60. Moreover concerning the stranger that is not of Thy people Israel, when he shall come out of a far country for Thy name's sake—for they shall hear of Thy great name, and of Thy mighty hand, and of Thine out-stretched arm—when he shall come and pray toward this house; hear Thou in heaven Thy dwelling-place, and do according to all that the stranger calleth to Thee for; that all the peoples of the earth may know Thy name, to fear Thee, as doth Thy people Israel, and that they may know that Thy name is called upon this house which I have built.

And let these my words, wherewith I have made supplication before the LORD, be nigh unto the LORD our God day and night, that He maintain the cause of His servant, and the cause of His people Israel, as every day shall require; that all the peoples of the earth may know that the LORD, He is God; there is none else. [See the parallel passage in 2 Chronicles 6:32-33.]

Isaiah 2:2-4. And it shall come to pass in the end of days, that the mountain of the Lord's house shall be established as the top of the mountains, and shall be exalted above the hills; and all nations shall flow unto it. And many peoples shall go and say: "Come ye, and let us go up to the mountain of the LORD, To the house of the God of Jacob; and He will teach us of His ways, And we will walk in His paths." For out of Zion shall go forth the law, and the word of the LORD from Jerusalem. And He shall judge between the nations, and shall decide for many peoples; and they shall beat their swords into plowshares, and their spears into pruning-hooks; nation shall not lift up sword against nation, neither shall they learn war any more.

Isaiah 45:22. Look unto Me, and be ye saved, all the ends of the earth; for I am God, and there is none else.

Isaiah 56:6-7. Also the aliens, that join themselves to the LORD, to minister unto Him, and to love the name of the LORD, to be His servants, every one that keepeth the sabbath from profaning it, and holdeth fast by My covenant: even them will I bring to My holy mountain, and make them joyful in My house of prayer; their burnt-offerings and their sacrifices shall be acceptable upon Mine altar; for My house shall be called a house of prayer for all peoples.

Zephaniah 2:11. The LORD will be terrible unto them; for He will famish all the gods of the earth; then shall all the isles of the nations worship Him, every one from its place.

Zephaniah 3:9. For then will I turn to the peoples a pure language, that they may all call upon the name of the LORD, to serve Him with one consent.

Zechariah 14:16-19. And it shall come to pass, that every one that is left of all the nations that came against Jerusalem shall go up from year to year to worship the King, the LORD of hosts, and to keep the feast of tabernacles. And it shall be, that whoso of the families of the earth goeth not up unto Jerusalem to worship the King, the LORD of hosts, upon them there shall be no rain. And if the family of Egypt go not up, and come not, they shall have no over-flow; there shall be the plague, wherewith the LORD will smite the nations that go not up to keep the feast of tabernacles. This shall be the punishment of Egypt, and the punishment of all the nations that go not up to keep the feast of tabernacles.

Malachi 1:11. For from the rising of the sun even unto the going down of the same My name is great among the nations; and in every place offerings are presented unto My name, even pure oblations; for My name is great among the nations, saith the LORD of hosts.

Psalm 86:9. All nations whom Thou hast made shall come and prostrate themselves before Thee, O LORD; and they shall glorify Thy name.

Psalm 117. O praise the LORD, all ye nations; laud Him, all ye peoples. For His mercy is great toward us; and the truth of the LORD endureth for ever. Hallelujah.

GENTILES IN TANACH WHO WORSHIPED THE GOD OF ISRAEL

Melchizedek, King of Salem (Genesis 14:18-20). And Mel-chizedek king of Salem brought forth bread and wine; and he was priest of God the Most High. And he blessed him [Abram], and said: "Blessed be Abram of God Most High, Maker of heaven and earth; and blessed be God the Most

High, who hath delivered thine enemies into thy hand."
And he gave him a tenth of all.

Jethro, the father-in-law of Moses (Exodus 18:9-12). And
Jethro rejoiced for all the goodness which the LORD had
done to Israel, in that He had delivered them out of the
hand of the Egyptians. And Jethro said: "Blessed be the
LORD, who hath delivered you out of the hand of the Egyptians, and out of the hand of Pharaoh; who hath delivered
the people from under the hand of the Egyptians. Now I
know that the LORD is greater than all gods; yea, for that
they dealt proudly against them." And Jethro, Moses'
father-in-law, took a burnt-offering and sacrifices for God;
and Aaron came, and all the elders of Israel, to eat bread
with Moses' father-in-law before God.

*Ruth the Moabitess, ancestress of King David (Ruth 1:15-
17; 4:13, 21-22).* And she [Naomi] said: "Behold, thy sister-
in-law is gone back unto her people, and unto her god;
return thou after thy sister-in-law." And Ruth said:
"Entreat me not to leave thee, and to return from following
after thee; for whither thou goest, I will go; and where thou
lodgest, I will lodge; thy people shall be my people, and thy
God my God; where thou diest, will I die, and there will I
be buried; the LORD do so to me, and more also, if aught
but death part thee and me."

So Boaz took Ruth, and she became his wife; and he
went in unto her, and the LORD gave her conception, and
she bore a son . . . and Boaz begot Obed; and Obed begot
Jesse, and Jesse begot David.

The People of Nineveh (Jonah 3:3-10). So Jonah arose,
and went unto Nineveh, according to the word of the
LORD. Now Nineveh was an exceeding great city, of three

days' journey. And Jonah began to enter into the city a day's journey, and he proclaimed, and said: "Yet forty days, and Nineveh shall be overthrown."

And the people of Nineveh believed God; and they proclaimed a fast, and put on sackcloth, from the greatest of them even to the least of them. And the tidings reached the king of Nineveh, and he arose from his throne, and laid his robe from him, and covered him with sackcloth, and sat in ashes. And he caused it to be proclaimed and published through Nineveh by the decree of the king and his nobles, saying: "Let neither man nor beast, herd nor flock, taste any thing; let them not feed, nor drink water; but let them be covered with sackcloth, both man and beast, and let them cry mightily unto God; yea, let them turn every one from his evil way, and from the violence that is in their hands. Who knoweth whether God will not turn and repent, and turn away from His fierce anger, that we perish not?" And God saw their works, that they turned from their evil way; and God repented of the evil, which He said He would do unto them; and He did it not.

IN THE NEW TESTAMENT

Luke 2:25-32. And behold, there was a man in Jerusalem whose name was Simeon; and this man was righteous and devout, looking for the consolation of Israel; and the Holy Spirit was upon him. And it had been revealed to him by the Holy Spirit that he would not see death before he had seen the Lord's Christ. And he came in the Spirit into the temple; and when the parents brought in the child Jesus, to carry out for Him the custom of the Law, then he took Him into his arms, and blessed God, and said, "Now Lord, Thou dost let Thy bond-servant depart in peace, according to Thy word; for my eyes have seen Thy salvation, which Thou hast prepared in the presence of all peoples, A LIGHT OF REVELATION TO THE GENTILES, and the glory of Thy people Israel."

Romans 15:7-12. Accept one another, just as Christ also accepted us to the glory of God. For I say that Christ has become a servant to the circumcision on behalf of the truth of God to confirm the promises given to the fathers, and for the Gentiles to glorify God for His mercy, as it is written, "THEREFORE I WILL GIVE PRAISE TO THEE AMONG THE GENTILES, AND I WILL SING TO THY NAME." And again he says, "REJOICE, O GENTILES, WITH HIS PEOPLE." And again, "PRAISE THE LORD ALL YOU GENTILES, AND LET ALL THE PEOPLES PRAISE HIM." And again Isaiah says, "THERE SHALL COME THE ROOT OF JESSE, AND HE WHO ARISES TO RULE OVER THE GENTILES, IN HIM SHALL THE GENTILES HOPE." [Quoting from, respectively, Psalm 18:49; Deuteronomy 32:43; Psalm 117:1; Isaiah 11:10.]

Ephesians 2:11-22. Therefore remember that formerly you, the Gentiles in the flesh, who are called "Uncircumcised" by the so-called "Circumcision," which is performed in the flesh by human hands—remember that you were at that time separate from Christ, excluded from the commonwealth of Israel, and strangers to the covenants of promise, having no hope and without God in the world. But now in Christ Jesus you who formerly were far off have been brought near by the blood of Christ. For He Himself is our peace, who made both groups into one, and broke down the barrier of the dividing wall, by abolishing in His flesh

94

the enmity, which is the Law of commandments contained in ordinances, that in Himself He might make the two into one new man, thus establishing peace, and might reconcile them both in one body to God through the cross, by it having put to death the enmity. AND HE CAME AND PREACHED PEACE TO YOU WHO WERE FAR AWAY, AND PEACE TO THOSE WHO WERE NEAR; for through Him we both have our access in one Spirit to the Father. So then, you are no longer strangers and aliens, but you are fellow citizens with the saints, and are of God's household, having been built upon the foundation of the apostles and prophets, Christ Jesus Himself being the cornerstone, in whom the whole building, being fitted together is growing into a holy temple in the Lord; in whom you also are being built together into a dwelling of God in the Spirit.

APPENDIX 5
Portions of Tanach Quoted in the New Testament

The following passages of Tanach are quoted or referred to in the New Testament, either according to the Masoretic* text or the Septuagint.* Sometimes the quotation differs from either, due to the variety in textual traditions available in the New Testament era as well as to freedoms allowed in the citation of Scripture passages. This is not an exhaustive listing.

The following abbreviations have been used:

Tanach	New Testament
Gen. = Genesis	Matt. = Matthew
Exod. = Exodus	Rom. = Romans
Lev. = Leviticus	1 Cor. = 1 Corinthians
Num. = Numbers	2 Cor. = 2 Corinthians
Deut. = Deuteronomy	Gal. = Galatians
Judg. = Judges	Eph. = Ephesians
2 Sam. = 2 Samuel	2 Tim. = 2 Timothy
Isa. = Isaiah	Heb. = Hebrews
Jer. = Jeremiah	1 Pet. = 1 Peter
Hos. = Hosea	2 Pet. = 2 Peter
Hab. = Habakkuk	
Hag. = Haggai	
Zech. = Zechariah	

Mal. = Malachi
Ps. = Psalms
Prov. = Proverbs
Dan. = Daniel

? = possibly a quotation

Gen. 2:2.	Heb. 4:4	*Exod. 3:6.*	Matt. 22:32
Gen. 2:7.	1 Cor. 15:45		Mark 12:26
Gen. 2:24.	Matt. 19:5		Luke 20:37
	Mark 10:7f.		Acts 7:32
	1 Cor. 6:16	*Exod. 3:12.*	Acts 7:7*b*
	Eph. 5:31	*Exod. 9:16.*	Rom. 9:17
Gen. 12:1.	Acts 7:3	*Exod. 12:46.*	John 19:36
Gen. 12:3.	Acts 3:25	*Exod. 13:2, 12.*	Luke 2:23
	Gal. 3:8		
Gen. 13:15.	Gal. 3:16	*Exod. 16:18.*	2 Cor. 8:15
Gen. 15:5.	Rom. 4:18	*Exod. 19:5f.*	1 Pet. 2:9
Gen 15:6.	Rom. 4:3, 9, 22	*Exod. 19:13.*	Heb. 12:20
		Exod. 20:5.	James 4:5
	Gal. 3:6	*Exod. 20:12.*	Matt. 15:4
	James 2:23*a*		Mark 7:10
Gen 15:13f.	Acts 7:6f.		Eph. 6:2
Gen. 15:18.	Gal. 3:16	*Exod. 20:12-16.*	Matt. 19:18f.
Gen. 17:5.	Rom. 4:17		Mark 10:19
Gen. 17:8.	Gal. 3:16		Luke 18:20
Gen. 18:10, 14.	Rom. 9:9	*Exod. 20:13.*	Matt. 5:21
			James 2:11*b*
Gen. 18:18.	Acts 3:25	*Exod. 20:13-17.*	Rom. 13:9
Gen. 21:10.	Gal. 4:30		
	Heb. 11:18	*Exod. 20:14.*	Matt. 5:27
Gen. 22:17.	Heb. 6:14		James 2:11*a*
?Gen. 22:18.	Gal. 3:16	*Exod. 20:17.*	Rom. 7:7
Gen. 25:23.	Rom. 9:12	*Exod. 21:17.*	Matt. 15:4
	Acts 3:25		Mark 7:10
		Exod. 21:24.	Matt. 5:38
Exod. 2:14.	Acts 7:27f.	*Exod. 22:27.*	Acts 23:5
Exod. 3:5, 7-10.	Acts 7:33f.	*Exod. 23:22.*	1 Pet. 2:9
		Exod. 24:8.	Heb. 9:20

Exod. 25:40.	Heb. 8:5	*Deut. 8:3.*	Matt. 4:4
Exod. 32:6.	1 Cor. 10:7		Luke 4:4
Exod. 33:19.	Rom. 9:15	*Deut. 9:19.*	Heb. 12:21
		Deut. 18:15.	Acts 3:22f.
Lev. 11:44.	1 Pet. 1:16		Acts 7:37
Lev. 12:8.	Luke 2:24	*Deut. 19:15.*	Matt. 18:16
Lev. 18:5.	Rom. 10:5		2 Cor. 13:1
	Gal. 3:12	*Deut. 21:23.*	Gal. 3:13
Lev. 19:2.	1 Pet. 1:16	*Deut. 24:1.*	Matt. 5:31
Lev. 19:18.	Matt. 5:43		
	Matt. 19:19	*?2 Sam. 7:14.*	2 Cor. 6:16-
	Matt. 22:39		18
	Mark 12:31	*2 Sam. 7:14.*	Heb. 1:5b
	Luke 10:27		
	Rom. 13:9	*1 Kings 19:14.*	Rom. 11:3
	Gal. 5:14	*1 Kings 19:18.*	Rom. 11:4
	James 2:8		
Lev. 20:7.	1 Pet. 1:16	*Isa. 1:9.*	Rom. 9:29
Lev. 24:20.	Matt. 5:38	*Isa. 6:9f.*	Matt. 13:13-
Lev. 26:11f.	2 Cor. 6:16		15
			Mark 4:12
Deut. 5:16.	Matt. 15:4		Luke 8:10
	Mark 7:10		John 12:40
	Eph. 6:2f.		Acts 28:26f.
Deut. 5:16-20.	Matt. 19:18f.	*Isa. 7:14.*	Matt. 1:23
	Mark 10:19	*Isa. 8:14.*	Rom. 9:33
Deut. 5:17.	Matt. 5:21		1 Pet. 2:8
	James 2:11b	*Isa. 8:17.*	Heb. 2:13a
Deut. 5:17-21.	Rom. 13:9	*Isa. 8:18.*	Heb. 2:13b
Deut. 5:18.	Matt. 5:27	*Isa. 9:1.*	Matt. 4:15f
	James 2:11a	*Isa. 10:22f.*	Rom. 9:27f.
Deut. 5:21.	Rom. 7:7	*Isa. 11:10.*	Rom. 15:12
Deut. 6:4f.	Matt. 22:37	*Isa. 12:3.*	John 7:38
	Mark 12:29f.	*Isa. 22:13.*	1 Cor. 15:32
	Luke 10:27	*Isa. 25:8.*	1 Cor. 15:54f.
Deut. 6:13.	Matt. 4:10	*Isa. 26:19.*	Eph. 5:14
	Luke 4:8	*Isa. 27:9.*	Rom. 11:26f.
Deut. 6:16.	Matt. 4:7	*Isa. 28:11f.*	1 Cor. 14:21

Isa. 28:16.	Rom. 9:33	*Isa. 59:7f.*	Rom. 3:10-18
	Rom. 10:11	*Isa. 59:20f.*	Rom. 11:26f.
	1 Pet. 2:6	*Isa. 60:1.*	Eph. 5:14
Isa. 29:10.	Rom. 11:8	*Isa. 61:1f.*	Luke 4:18f.
Isa. 29:13.	Matt. 15:8f.	*Isa. 62:11.*	Matt. 21:5
	Mark 7:6f.	*Isa. 64:4.*	1 Cor. 2:9
Isa. 29:14.	1 Cor. 1:19	*Isa. 65:1f.*	Rom. 10:20f.
Isa. 40:3.	Matt. 3:3	*Isa. 66:1f.*	Acts 7:49f.
	Mark 1:2f.		
Isa. 40:3-5.	Luke 3:4–6	*Jer. 7:11.*	Matt. 21:13
Isa. 40:6-8.	1 Pet. 1:24f.		Mark 11:17
Isa. 40:13.	Rom. 11:34f.		Luke 19:46
	1 Cor. 2:16	*Jer. 9:23.*	1 Cor. 1:31
Isa. 42:1-4.	Matt. 12:18-21	*Jer. 9:24.*	2 Cor. 10:17
		Jer. 31:15.	Matt. 2:18
Isa. 43:20f.	1 Pet. 2:9	*Jer. 31:31-34.*	Heb. 8:8-12
Isa. 44:3.	John 7:38	*Jer. 31:33.*	John 6:45
Isa. 45:23.	Rom. 14:11		Heb. 10:16
Isa. 49:6.	Acts 13:47	*Jer. 31:34.*	Heb. 10:17
Isa. 49:8.	2 Cor. 6:2		
Isa. 52:5.	Rom. 2:24	*Hos. 2:25.*	Rom. 9:25f.
Isa. 52:7.	Rom. 10:15	*Hos. 6:6.*	Matt. 9:13
Isa. 52:11f.	2 Cor. 6:16-18		Matt. 12:7
		Hos. 10:8.	Luke 23:30
Isa. 52:15.	Rom. 15:21	*Hos. 11:1.*	Matt. 2:15
Isa. 53:1.	John 12:38	*Hos. 13:14.*	1 Cor. 15:54f.
	Rom. 10:16		
Isa. 53:4.	Matt. 8:17	*Joel 3:1-5.*	Acts 2:17-21
Isa. 53:4-6, 9.	1 Pet. 2:22-24	*Joel 3:5.*	Rom. 10:13
Isa. 53:7f.	Acts 8:32f.		
Isa. 53:12.	Luke 22:37	*Amos 5:25-27.*	Acts 7:42f.
Isa. 54:1.	Gal. 4:27	*Amos 9:11f.*	Acts 15:16-18
Isa. 54:13.	John 6:45		
Isa. 55:3.	Acts 13:34	*Hab. 1:5.*	Acts 13:41
Isa. 56:7.	Matt. 21:13	*Hab. 2:3f.*	Heb. 10:37f.
	Mark 11:17	*Hab. 2:4.*	Rom. 1:17
	Luke 19:46		Gal. 3:11
Isa. 58:11.	John 7:38	*Hab. 2:6.*	Heb. 12:26

Zech. 9:9.	Matt. 21:5	*Ps. 41:10.*	John 13:18
	John 12:15	*Ps. 44:23.*	Rom. 8:36
Zech. 11:12f.	Matt. 27:9f.	*Ps. 45:7f.*	Heb. 1:8f.
Zech. 12:10.	John 19:37	*Ps. 51:6.*	Rom. 3:4
Zech. 13:7.	Matt. 26:31	*Ps. 68:19.*	Eph. 4:8
	Mark 14:27	*Ps. 69:5.*	John 15:25
		Ps. 69:10.	John 2:17
			Rom. 15:3
Mal. 1:2f.	Rom. 9:13	*Ps. 69:23f.*	Rom. 11:9f.
Mal. 3:1.	Matt. 11:10.	*Ps. 69:26.*	Acts 1:20
	Mark 1:2f.	*Ps. 78:2.*	Matt. 13:35
	Luke 7:27	*Ps. 82:6.*	John 10:34
		Ps. 94:11.	1 Cor. 3:20
Ps. 2:1f.	Acts 4:25f.	*Ps. 95:7f.*	Heb. 3:15
Ps. 2:7.	Acts 13:33		Heb. 4:7
	Heb. 1:5*a*		
	Heb. 5:5	*Ps. 95:7-11.*	Heb. 3:7-11
Ps. 5:10.	Rom. 3:10–18	*Ps. 95:11.*	Heb. 4:3, 5
Ps. 8:3.	Matt. 21:16	*?Ps. 97:7.*	Heb. 1:6
Ps. 8:5-7.	Heb. 2:6-8	*Ps. 102:26-28.*	Heb. 1:10-12
Ps. 8:6.	Cor. 15:27	*Ps. 104:4.*	Heb. 1:7
Ps. 10:7.	Rom. 3:10-18	*Ps. 109:8.*	Acts 1:20
Ps. 14:1-3.	Rom. 3:10-18	*Ps. 110:1.*	Matt. 22:44
Ps. 16:8-11.	Acts 2:25-28		Mark 12:36
Ps. 16:10.	Acts 13:35		Luke 20:42f.
Ps. 18:50.	Rom. 15:9		Acts 2:34f.
Ps. 19:5.	Rom. 10:18		Heb. 1:3
Ps. 22:2.	Matt. 27:46	*Ps. 110:4.*	Heb. 5:6
	Mark 15:34		Heb. 7:17, 21
Ps. 22:19.	John 19:24	*Ps. 112:9.*	2 Cor. 9:9
Ps. 22:23.	Heb. 2:12	*Ps. 116:10.*	2 Cor. 4:13
Ps. 24:1.	1 Cor. 10:26	*Ps. 117:1.*	Rom. 15:11
Ps. 31:6.	Luke 23:46	*Ps. 118:6.*	Heb. 13:6
Ps. 32:1f.	Rom. 4:7f.	*Ps. 118:22.*	Acts 4:11
Ps. 34:12-16.	1 Pet. 3:10-12		1 Pet. 2:7
Ps. 34:20.	John 19:36	*Ps. 118:22f.*	Matt. 21:42
Ps. 35:19.	John 15:25		Mark 12:10f.
Ps. 36:2.	Rom. 3:10-18		Luke 20:17
Ps. 40:7-9.	Heb. 10:5-7		

100

Ps. 118:26.	Matt. 23:39	*Prov. 26:11.*	2 Pet. 2:22
	Luke 13:35		
Ps. 140:4.	Rom. 3:10-18	*Job. 5:13.*	1 Cor. 3:19
		Job. 41:3.	Rom. 11:34f.
Prov. 3:11f.	Heb. 12:5f.		
Prov. 3:34.	James 4:6	*Dan. 9:27.*	Matt. 24:15
	1 Pet. 5:5		Mark 13:14
Prov. 11:31.	1 Pet. 4:18	*Dan. 12:11.*	Matt. 24:15
Prov. 25:21f.	Rom. 12:19f.		Mark 13:14

APPENDIX 6
Jesus and Christians Outside the New Testament

Josephus, *Jewish Antiquities* (c. 93 C.E.). The Jewish historian Josephus has written a passage that contains some later interpolations. The following paragraph brackets the probable interpolations and is followed by a suggested original rendering by Joseph Klausner, late professor at Hebrew University in Jerusalem.

Now, there was about this time Jesus, a wise man [if it be lawful to call him a man], for he was a doer of wonderful works, a teacher of such men as receive the truth with pleasure. He drew over to him both many of the Jews, and many of the Gentiles. [He was the Messiah.] And when Pilate, at the suggestion of the principal men amongst us, had condemned him to the cross, those that loved him at the first did not forsake him [for he appeared to them alive again at the third day; as the divine prophets had foretold these and ten thousand other wonderful things concerning him]. And the tribe of Christians, so named from him, are not extinct at this day.[1]

And Prof. Klausner's suggested rendering:

Now, there was about this time Jesus, a wise man; for he was a doer of wonderful works, a teacher of such men as receive the truth with pleasure. He drew over to him both many of the Jews and many of the Gentiles. And when Pilate, at the suggestion of the principal men among us, had condemned him to the cross, those that loved him at the first ceased not so to do; and the race of Christians, so named from him, are not extinct even now.[2]

PLINY

Pliny the Younger, *Letter to Trajan* (c.111-117 C.E.). A letter from the imperial legate, or "governor," of the Roman province of Bithynia, to the Emperor Trajan at Rome:

... they maintained that their fault or error amounted to nothing more than this: they were in the habit of meeting on a certain fixed day before sunrise and reciting an antiphonal hymn to Christ as God, and binding themselves with an oath—not to commit any crime, but to abstain from all acts of theft, robbery and adultery, from breaches of faith, from repudiating a trust when called upon to honour it. . . .[3]

---

1. *Antiquities xviii.33* (early second century) from F.F. Bruce, *Jesus and Christian Origins Outside the New Testament* (Grand Rapids: Eerdmans, 1974), p. 37.
2. J. Klausner, *Jesus of Nazareth* (London, 1929), p. 55ff.
3. Pliny, *Epistles* x.96, from Bruce, p. 26.

Tacitus, *Roman Annals* (c.115-117 C.E.). From the histories of a Roman chronicler:

> They got their name from Christ, who was executed by sentence of the procurator Pontius Pilate in the reign of Tiberius. That checked the pernicious superstition for a short time, but it broke out afresh—not only in Judea, where the plague first arose, but in Rome itself, where all the horrible and shameful things in the world collect and find a home.[4]

SUETONIUS

Suetonius, *Life of Claudius* (c.120 C.E.). From the pen of another Roman historian noted for his biographies of the early Roman emperors:

> He expelled the Jews from Rome, on account of the riots in which they were constantly indulging, at the instigation of Chrestus.[5]

SANHEDRIN

Sanhedrin 43*a* (200-500 C.E.). From the pages of the Babylonian Talmud. Bracketed portions belong to the actual Soncino edition translation.

On the eve of the Passover Yeshu[6] was hanged. For forty days before the execution took place, a herald went forth and cried, "He is going forth to be stoned because he has prac-

---

4. Tacitus, *Annals* xv.44, from Bruce, p. 22.
5. Suetonius, *Claudius* 25.4, from Bruce, p. 21.
6. A Talmudic designation of Jesus.

tised sorcery and enticed Israel to apostacy. Any one who can say anything in his favour, let him come forward and plead on his behalf." But since nothing was brought forward in his favour he was hanged on the eve of Passover!—Ulla retorted: Do you suppose that he was one for whom a defence could be made? Was he not a *Mesith* [enticer], concerning whom Scripture says, *Neither shalt thou spare, neither shalt thou conceal him?*[7] With Yeshu however it was different, for he was connected with the government [or royalty, i.e., influential].[8]

7. Deuteronomy 13:9.
8. "Sanhedrin," vol. 3 of *Nezikin,* Babylonian Talmud, edited by Isidore Epstein, reprint (London: Soncino, 1938), p. 281.

APPENDIX 7
The Early Jewish Christians and the Jewish Community

The first Jewish believers in Jesus were originally considered to be a sect within Judaism, which was as varied as modern Judaism. The sect of the "Nazarenes" existed alongside the Pharisees, the Sadducees, the Essenes, and the Zealots. In the earliest days, they would have been in disfavor more with the Sadducees, who represented the "establishment," than with the Pharisees; the situation changed, however, with the destruction of the Temple and the emergence of Pharisaism as "mainline" Judaism.

All believers, Jewish or Gentile, were considered part of Judaism by the Roman authorities as well. They were accorded whatever toleration or lack thereof was given to Judaism.

In the beginning, the church was composed strictly of Jews. The first leader of the church was James, the brother of Jesus, who was killed in 62 C.E. A rather poetic description of him given by Hegesippus has come down to us. It is uncertain how much of this tradition is trustworthy.

[He was] holy from his birth; he drank no wine or strong

drink, neither did he eat flesh. No razor came near his head; he did not anoint himself with oil or go to the baths. He alone was permitted to enter the sanctuary, for he wore garments of linen, not of wool; he would enter the Temple alone and was often found on his knees praying for forgiveness for the (Jewish) people.... Because of his unsurpassed righteousness he was called "the Just" and ... "Bulwark of the People."[1]

Eusebius, the great fourth-century historian, tells us that the Jewish Christians, who were largely concentrated in Jerusalem, scattered to the city of Pella or to the other side of the Jordan some time after the killing of James.[2] Many, however, stayed behind. It is thought that the Jewish Christians fled to Pella during a lift in the Roman seige of 68-70 C.E. That would have been in response to Jesus' words:

"When you see Jerusalem surrounded by armies, you will know that its desolation is near. Then let those who are in Judea flee to the mountains...."[3]

The Jewish Christians did not participate in the war against Rome, but not due to lack of patriotism. The Romans, after all, were increasing their persecution of Jewish Christians. Domitian arrested two grandsons of Jude, although they were later released; and Trajan killed the second Jerusalem church leader, Simon son of Cleophas.

The flight to Pella did not help relations with the Jewish community, and with the destruction of the Temple in 70 C.E., the road diverged even farther. While Pharisaic Juda-

1. Quoted in F. F. Bruce, *New Testament History* (Garden City, N.Y.: Anchor, 1972), pp. 369-70.
2. Jakob Jocz, *The Jewish People and Jesus Christ* (Grand Rapids: Baker, 1979), pp. 165-66.
3. Luke 21:20-21.

ism began establishing itself as "normative" Judaism, the Jewish Christians saw the destruction of the Temple as additional evidence that Jesus was the final atonement for sin. That, coupled with a policy of "open admission" for Gentiles into the church, put a strain on relations. It should be emphasized, however, that the early Jewish Christians continued to worship in the Temple and synagogues.

In the early period, we have the evidence of the book of Acts:

> One day Peter and John were going up to the temple at the time of prayer—at three in the afternoon.[4]

> As his custom was, Paul went into the synagogue, and on three Sabbath days he reasoned with them from the Scriptures.[5]

> Paul had decided to sail past Ephesus to avoid spending time in the province of Asia, for he was in a hurry to reach Jerusalem, if possible, by the day of Pentecost [*Shavuot;* for the required pilgrimage to the temple].[6]

From the later period, we find this in the gospel of John, generally dated c. 90 C.E.: "They will put you out of the synagogue."[7] That indicates that even at a late date, synagogue attendance was part of the worship of Jewish Christians.

We find a strange development in the synagogue liturgy near the end of the first century, as the threat to Judaism grew from within. Samuel the Small (d. c.125 C.E.) added a special "blessing" to the Eighteen Benedictions that was

---

4. Acts 3:1.
5. Acts 17:2.
6. Acts 20:16.
7. John 16:2.

not a blessing at all but a malediction against the *minim*. According to the Talmud:

> R. Levi said: The benediction relating to the *Minim* was instituted in Jabneh.... Our Rabbis taught: Simeon ha-Pakuli arranged the eighteen benedictions in order before Rabban Gamaliel in Jabneh. Said Rabban Gamaliel to the Sages: Can any one among you frame a benediction relating to the *Minim?* Samuel the Lesser arose and composed it.[8]

A recent rendition of this so-called *Birkat Haminim* (Blessing of the Heretics) runs as follows:

> And for slanderers let there be no hope, and let all wickedness perish as in a moment; let all thine enemies be speedily cut off, and the dominion of arrogance do thou uproot and crush, cast down and humble speedily in our days. Blessed art thou, O Lord, who breakest the enemies and humblest the arrogant.[9]

However, an older text from a Cairo genizah* reads:

> For the renegades let there be no hope, and may the arrogant kingdom soon be rooted out in our days, and the Nazarenes and the *minim* perish as in a moment and be blotted out from the book of life and with the righteous may they not be inscribed. Blessed art thou, O Lord, who humblest the arrogant.[10]

The question has been debated as to who the *minim* were. The older text quoted, as well as Rashi and others[11]

---

8. "Berakot," in *Zeraim*, Babylonian Talmud, edited by Isidore Epstein, reprint (London: Soncino, 1938), 8*b*-29*a*, p. 175.

9. *Singer's Authorized Prayer Book*, p. 48, quoted in Jocz, p. 53.

10. S. Schechter, "Genizah Specimens," *Jewish Quarterly Review* x., p. 657, quoted in Jocz, p. 53.

11. As noted in Jocz, pp. 53-54: quoting Rashi in a manuscript on *Berakot; Siddur of the Gaon Rab Amram* (1426 CE; Codex Bodl. 1095); *Mahzor* (Codex de Rossi Nr. 159 of Parma), p. 2.

show that the "Nazarenes," or Jewish Christians, were one of the groups referred to as *minim*. Jåkob Jocz, Professor Emeritus of Systematic Theology at Wycliffe College, University of Toronto, suspects that *minim* is a corruption of *ma'aminim,* "believers," referring to the Jewish Christians.[12] A Jewish Christian could hardly be expected to recite a prayer against himself; the *Birkat Haminim,* therefore, was an effective tool to dissociate the Jewish believers from the synagogue. It was not that they decided to leave—they were forced out by the leadership.

The attitude of mainstream Judaism to Jewish Christians is well illustrated by two Talmudic accounts that relate incidents of the late first to early second centuries C.E. The first account deals with a rabbi who found certain Christian teaching attractive; the second forbids medical treatment by a Jewish Christian, even though one may be at the point of death. The radical antagonism toward Jewish believers is evident. Bracketed portions and footnotes are in the original text of the Soncino translation.

Our Rabbis taught: When R. Eliezer was arrested because of *Minuth*[a] they brought him up to the tribune to be judged. Said the governor to him, "How can a sage man like you occupy himself with those idle things?" He replied, "I acknowledge the Judge as right." The governor thought that he referred to him—though he really referred to his Father in Heaven—and said, "Because thou hast acknowledged me as right, I pardon; thou art acquitted." When he came home, his disciples called on him to console him, but he would accept no consolation. Said R. Akiba to him, "Master, wilt thou permit me to say one thing of what thou hast taught me?" He replied, "Say it." "Master," said he, "perhaps some of the

12. Jocz, pp. 177-78.

teaching of the *Minim* had been transmitted to thee and thou didst approve of it and because of that thou was arrested?" He exclaimed: "Akiba thou hast reminded me." I was once walking in the upper-market of Sepphoris when I came across one [of the disciples of Jesus the Nazarene] Jacob of Kefar-Sekaniah[b] by name, who said to me: It is written in your Torah, *Thou shalt not bring the hire of a harlot . . . into the house of the Lord thy God.* May such money be applied to the erection of a retiring place for the High Priest? To which I made no reply. Said he to me: Thus was I taught [by Jesus the Nazarene], *For of the hire of a harlot hath she gathered them and unto the hire of a harlot shall they return: they came from a place of filth, let them go to a place of filth.* Those words pleased me very much, and that is why I was arrested for apostasy. . . .

[a] . . . "heresy," with special reference to Christianity. [During the Roman persecution of Christians in Palestine in the year 109 under Trajan . . . R. Eliezer b. Hyrcanus was arrested on suspicion of following that sect.]

[b] . . . this Jacob may have been either James the son of Alphaeus (Mark III,18) or James the Little (ibid. XV, 40).[13]

The second incident is as follows:

No man should have any dealings with *Minim,* nor is it allowed to be healed by them even [in risking] an hour's life. It once happened to Ben Dama the son of R. Ishmael's sister that he was bitten by a serpent and Jacob, a native of Kefar Sekaniah, came to heal him but R. Ishmael did not let him; whereupon Ben Dama said, "My brother R. Ishmael, let him, so that I may be healed by him: I will even cite a verse from the Torah that he is to be permitted"; but he did not manage to complete his saying, when his soul departed and he died. Whereupon R. Ishmael exclaimed, Happy art thou Ben Dama for thou wert pure in body and thy soul likewise left thee in purity; . . . It is different with the teaching of *Minim,*

13. "Abodah Zarah," vol. 4 of *Nezikin, Babylonian Talmud, 16b-17a,* p. 85.

for it draws, and one [having dealings with them] may be drawn after them.[14]

The decisive break in relations, however, occurred at the time of the Bar Kosiba revolt (132-135 C.E.) under the Emperor Hadrian. The revolt was prompted by Hadrian's ban on circumcision, and the Jewish Christians joined in that cause with fervor. In the middle of the revolt, though, Rabbi Akiba declared Bar Kosiba to be the Messiah in fulfillment of Numbers 24:17, "There shall step forth a star out of Jacob." As the word in Aramaic for "the star" is "*kochba*," Bar Kosiba's name became Bar Kochba, "son of the star."

At that point, the Jewish Christians could no longer support the war carried on under the auspices of "Messiah" Bar Kochba. So they once again pulled out. This time it led to the decisive break. An additional Talmudic passage, without a clear date but prior to the year 230 C.E., shows the continuing hardening of the lines. An admonition is given to allow the books of the Jewish Christians to be burned rather than be rescued in the event of a fire:

Come and hear: The blank spaces[a] and the Books of the Minim[b] may not be saved from a fire, but they must be burnt in their place, they and the Divine Names occurring in them. Now surely it means the blank portions of a Scroll of the Law? No: the blank spaces in the Books of Minim. Seeing that we may not save the Books of Minim themselves, need their blank spaces be stated?

[a]Jast. s.v ... translates, the gospels, though observing that here it is understood as blanks.
[b]Sectarians. The term denotes various kinds of Jewish

---

14. *Ibid.*, 27*b*, p. 137.

sectarians, such as the Sadducees, Samaritans, Judeo-Christians, etc., according to the date of the passage in which the term is used. The reference here is probably to the last-named.[15] ("Jast." is the Soncino abbreviation for M. Jastrow's *Dictionary of the Targumim, the Talmud Bible* [sic] *and Yerushalmi, and the Midrashic Literature.*)

The Bar Kochba revolt really marks the end of the early era of Jewish Christianity. After the complete separation from Jewish community life, Jewish Christians largely turned inward and developed unbiblical doctrines and lifestyles, or else were absorbed into the larger body of Gentile Christians. There were, however, some congregations of Jewish believers that exhibited a powerful testimony in the second and third centuries C.E.[16]

---

15. "Shabbath," vol. 1 of *Mo'ed*, Babylonian Talmud, 116*a*, p. 569.
16. See *The Church from the Circumcision* by Bagatti for the powerful testimony of Jewish believers in the second and third centuries C.E.

APPENDIX 8
Order of Books in Different Versions of the Bible

The Jewish versions of the Scriptures have arranged the order of the books according to three categories: Torah,* given to Moses by God at Sinai; Neviim,* Hebrew for "Prophets"; and finally, the Ketuvim,* or "Writings," to which all other scriptural books belong. The actual order of the books, however, has varied at different times in Jewish history. Thus in the Talmudic tractate *Baba Bathra 14b,* we read:

> Our Rabbis taught: The order of the Prophets is, Joshua, Judges, Samuel, Kings, Jeremiah, Ezekiel, Isaiah, and the Twelve Minor Prophets . . . The order of the Hagiographa[1] is Ruth, the Book of Psalms, Job, Prophets,[2] Ecclesiastes, Song of Songs, Lamentations, Daniel and the Scroll of Esther, Ezra and Chronicles.

The Septuagint* version, however, grouped the books as follows: historical (Genesis through Esther); poetic and "didactic," or instructional (Job through Song of Songs);

---

1. Another term for the Ketuvim, from the Greek for "holy writings."
2. An apparent error in the Soncino edition; "Proverbs" is likely meant.

and prophetic (Isaiah through Malachi). That is the order that is generally used today in versions that also incorporate the New Testament. Thus there have been different orders of books among the Jewish people at various times and places. The theory that the present arrangement reflects the date various books were written cannot be substantiated in view of the differing orders found in ancient times.

The contrasting orders are set out below:

Traditional Jewish Order As Followed Today	Versions Incorporating New Testament and Based on Septuagint	
THE TORAH	Genesis	Matthew
Genesis	Exodus	Mark
Exodus	Leviticus	Luke
Leviticus	Numbers	John
Numbers	Deuteronomy	Acts
Deuteronomy	Joshua	Romans
	Judges	1 Corinthians
THE PROPHETS	Ruth	2 Corinthians
Former Prophets	1 Samuel	Galatians
Joshua	2 Samuel	Ephesians
Judges	1 Kings	Philippians
1 Samuel	2 Kings	Colossians
2 Samuel	1 Chronicles	1 Thessalonians
1 Kings	2 Chronicles	2 Thessalonians
2 Kings	Ezra	1 Timothy
	Nehemiah	2 Timothy
Latter Prophets	Esther	Titus
Isaiah	Job	Philemon
Jeremiah	Psalms	Hebrews
Ezekiel	Proverbs	James

Hosea
Joel
Amos
Obadiah
Jonah
Micah
Nahum
Habakkuk
Zephaniah
Haggai
Zechariah
Malachi

THE WRITINGS
Psalms
Proverbs
Job
Song of Songs
Ruth
Lamentations
Ecclesiastes
Esther
Daniel
Ezra
Nehemiah
1 Chronicles
2 Chronicles

Ecclesiastes
Song of Songs
Isaiah
Jeremiah
Lamentations
Ezekiel
Daniel
Hosea
Joel
Amos
Obadiah
Jonah
Micah
Nahum
Habakkuk
Zephaniah
Haggai
Zechariah
Malachi

1 Peter
2 Peter
1 John
2 John
3 John
Jude
Revelation

APPENDIX 9
Explanation of Terms

The terms marked in the text or appendixes by an asterisk will be found below in alphabetical order.

Alexander the Great. King of Macedon who overthrew the Persian Empire in 336 B.C.E. and launched the Greek and Roman eras upon which our modern western civilization is based. He died in 323. It was due to Alexander's influence in particular that "hellenization" came to play such a role in the succeeding centuries, where many things were modeled after the Greek way of life.

Amarna tablets. Cuneiform (wedge-like writing) clay tablets discovered at Tell el-Amarna, Egypt in 1887. They relate to political events in Judea and Syria from 1400-1360 B.C.E.

Antiochus III. Ruler over Asia Minor (modern-day Turkey), Syria, and Judea* from 223-187 B.C.E., as one of the three ruling families that took over from Alexander the Great. He lost most of his territory to Rome in 189.

Antiochus IV Epiphanes. Ruled 175-164 B.C.E. He is best known for attempting to hellenize Israel by stopping the Temple offerings and sacrificing a pig on the altar. This led to the famed Maccabean revolt and the institution of Hanukkah* commemorating the rededication of the Temple.

Antipas. Son of Herod the Great.* He received parts of

117

his father's kingdom after his death. He inherited regions around the Sea of Galilee and east of the Jordan River with the title of tetrarch.* By intrigue, he was deposed and exiled by Rome in 39 C.E.

Apocalyptic. A genre of literature that flourished especially between 200 B.C.E. and 100 C.E., in the period following the post-exilic prophets. Apocalyptic style can be found earlier, though, in the book of Daniel and in portions of Isaiah. Nonbiblical apocalyptic writing is characterized by pseudonymity (use of the name of a famous ancient figure as the ostensible author); the utilization of sometimes bizarre symbolism; the rewriting of history as prophecy; the portraying of the coming future age of God's kingdom as being on a schedule entirely uninfluenced by the actions of human beings; an overriding pessimism concerning the possibility of effecting social changes; and the recession of morality into the background as a motivation for religious actions. But it is noteworthy that apocalyptic literature in both the Tanach and the New Testament does not share in most of these characteristics. Biblical apocalyptic writing is realistically hopeful, ethically motivated, written by authors who identify themselves, and truly prophetic of the future. Yet its emphasis on God's ultimate intervention in history and its use of symbolism tends to identify it as belonging to this genre.

Apocrypha. Refers to a number of books not considered part of the Bible by Jews or Protestants, though they are accepted by Roman Catholics. Except for 2 Esdras, they are contained in editions of the Septuagint,* although this does not necessarily mean that Greek-speaking Jews thought them inspired. The apocryphal books of Maccabees contain the well-known story of Hanukkah.* Other books are theology, history, and legend, and are written in both prose and poetry. The following writings, with their probable dates of composition, are considered to belong to the apocrypha:

Book	Century
1 Esdras	2nd B.C.E.
2 Esdras	1st-3rd C.E.
Tobit	2nd B.C.E.
Judith	2nd B.C.E.
The Additions to Esther	2nd-1st B.C.E.
The Wisdom of Solomon	1st B.C.E.
Ecclesiasticus (The Wisdom of Jesus son of Sirach)	2nd B.C.E.
Baruch	2nd-1st B.C.E.
The Letter of Jeremiah	4th(?) or 2nd (?) B.C.E.
The Prayer of Azariah and the Song of the Three Young Men	2nd-1st B.C.E.
Susanna	2nd-1st B.C.E.
Bel and the Dragon	2nd-1st B.C.E.
The Prayer of Manasseh	2nd-1st (?) B.C.E.
1 Maccabees	c.140 B.C.E. (chapters 14-16, after 70 [?] C.E.)
2 Maccabees	1st B.C.E.
3 Maccabees	1st B.C.E.
4 Maccabees	20-54 C.E.
Psalm 151	(?) B.C.E.

Aramaic. A language closely related to Hebrew, Aramaic was spoken in the ancient Near East from as early as the ninth century B.C.E. Portions of Daniel (2:4–7:28) and Ezra (4:8–6:18; 7:12-26) as well as a verse of Jeremiah (10:11) and two words of Genesis (31:47) are in Aramaic. By the time of Jesus, it was the daily language of Jews living in Judea. The paraphrases of the Hebrew Scriptures called the Targums* are in Aramaic. Jesus Himself would likely have spoken in Aramaic. Dialects of the language survive to this day in the Middle East.

Archelaus. Son of Herod the Great* who ruled Judea* from 4 B.C.E. to 6 C.E. with the title of ethnarch* until he was deposed by Rome in order to stave off a revolt against his authority.

Bethlehem Ephrathah. A city south of Jerusalem, earlier called simply Ephrath. Its full name distinguishes it from a second Bethlehem in the north, seven miles northwest of Nazareth. Bethlehem Ephrathah was also known as the "City of David" since the ancestors of King David lived there.

Caesar Augustus. Also known as Octavian, he was the first of the line of "Caesars," a Roman family that ruled from 31 B.C.E. to Nero's death in 68 C.E.

Canon. A body of religious writings held to constitute the fixed unit of divine communication, and which is not open to addition or subtraction. Its authority in the life of the believer is by virtue of its being the revelation of God or the deity.

Conversion. See Appendix 3.

Documentary Hypothesis. The prevailing view that individual books in the Tanach,* and especially the Torah,* are each composed of several documents from different time periods which have been woven together. Documents of the Torah, for example, are held to actually come from a much later period than that of Moses. Kenneth A. Kitchen, Lecturer in Egyptian and Coptic at the University of Liverpool in England, however, writes that ". . . the documentary theory in its many variations has throughout been elaborated *in a vacuum,* without any proper reference to the Ancient

120

Oriental literatures to find out whether they had been created in this singular manner.... Now, nowhere in the Ancient Orient is there anything which is definitely known to parallel the elaborate history of fragmentary composition and conflation of Hebrew literature ... as the documentary hypotheses would postulate. And conversely, any attempt to apply the criteria of the documentary theorists to Ancient Oriental compositions that have known histories but exhibit the same literary phenomena results in manifest absurdities."[1]

Ethnarch. The title of Archelaus,* one of the sons of Herod the Great,* with a rough translation value of "governor" or "head of an ethnic community." It was used by Josephus as a title for subordinate rulers, particularly of peoples under foreign control. It was applied to the official in charge of Damascus (part of the Roman Empire).

*Genizah.** A special room of ancient synagogues. It was used by Jewish people for the disposal of wornout and therefore unusable holy books. The genizah of an ancient synagogue in Cairo is one of the prime sources of early medieval Jewish documents, the earliest being possibly eighth century C.E. Most of the early research on its material was done by Solomon Schechter, who traveled to Cairo in 1896 and brought back 100,000 pages of manuscripts to study at Cambridge University.

Hanukkah. The festival commemorating the victory of the Maccabees* over Antiochus Epiphanes* and specifically the rededication of the Temple altar. According to legend, when the Maccabees* retook the Temple, they

---

1. Kenneth A. Kitchen, *Ancient Orient and Old Testament* (Downers Grove, Ill: Inter-Varsity 1966), pp. 114-15.

found a cruse of oil sufficient to burn for only a day, yet it miraculously lasted for eight days. Hence the festival lasts eight days. Occurring in November or December, its history is recorded in the apocryphal* books of Maccabees.* Hanukkah is also mentioned once in the New Testament (John 10:22), called there by its Greek equivalent, the Festival of Dedication. The holiday waned in popularity following the crushing defeat by Rome, but it has recently become one of the most popular holidays among modern Jews.

Hasmoneans. See *Maccabees.*

Herod the Great. "King of the Jews" from 37 to 4 B.C.E. An Idumean, he was in part descended from the ancient Edomites, traditional enemies of Israel. The title "King of the Jews" was, as might be suspected, not conferred on him by Jews but by Rome, who by that time was the overlord of Judea.* Herod is infamous for his cruelty, which included wiping out the entire Hasmonean* ruling family. He is also noted for beginning a magnificent expansion of the Temple in 19 B.C.E. Because of his descent as well as his general behavior, he was very much hated by his Jewish subjects.

Judea. This is the designation of the entire land of Israel at the beginning of the Greco-Roman period. After the Roman Empire became established, "Judea" came to refer only to the southern portion of the area, while the northern portion was Galilee and the area in between was designated Samaria. This is the geography encountered in the New Testament. The term *Judea* should not be confused with *Judah*, referring to the southern kingdom of the Jewish people in biblical days. In writings by non-Jews, Judea in its widest sense as the equivalent of the entire land is often called Palestine.

Ketuvim. The "Writings," the third category of the Hebrew Scriptures. For a listing of its contents, see Appendix 8.

Last Supper. The meal Jesus and His disciples ate before He was put to death. It was a Passover Seder.

Maccabees. The name (derived from the Greek) of the family descended from Matthathias that revolted against Antiochus IV.* The name perhaps means "the hammerer." The family name was also called Hashmon; thus the Maccabees are also called "Hasmoneans." Judah Maccabee is the most famous as the leader of the revolt. As a result of the Maccabean revolt, Israel again became an independent nation from 152 to 37 B.C.E. After Judah's death in 161 B.C.E. his brother Jonathan took over. One of the Seleucids, Alexander Balas, appointed him high priest in 153 and civil ruler in 150. Jonathan was murdered in 143, and another Maccabee brother, Simon, became both ruler and high priest of Judea. He too was murdered in 135. Toward the end of Hasmonean domination, the early idealism waned. As a case in point, Alexander Jannaeus, the grandson of Simon Maccabee, ruled from 103-76. So tyrannical was he, that one Sukkot,* people at the Temple reportedly hurled their *etrogim* (citrons) at him as he officiated as high priest at the festival. Most horrible of all, he crucified 800 of his fellow Jews as rebels and murdered their families as they watched from the crosses. The modern festival of Hanukkah* recalls the early Maccabean heroism as a still-living ideal.

Masoretic text. From 500-1000 C.E., a group of scribes called the Masoretes worked on the Hebrew text of the Bible, faithfully transcribing, adding vowels, and making countless notes about details of the text. Their product is the standard Hebrew Bible used today. On the whole, the Masoretic text is the closest we can approach to the original writings, so faithfully was the Masoretic manuscript tradition handed down from generation to generation.

Mikveh. Traditional immersion in water for various ceremonial reasons. See Appendix 2.

Nebuchadnezzar. Also *Nebuchadrezzar.* King of Babylon from 605-562 B.C.E. In 605 he subjugated both Syria and Judah, and Jerusalem in 597. In 587 Jerusalem was sacked. All those times there were deportations to Babylon, as possibly again in 582. After that, Nebuchadnezzar invaded Egypt and in later years built up the city of Babylon.

Neviim. The prophetic portion of the Hebrew Scriptures, it is divided into the Former Prophets and the Latter Prophets. For a listing of its content, see Appendix 8.

Pharaoh. Common title for the ancient kings of Egypt, beginning around 1450 B.C.E. The pharaoh of the Exodus is thought to have been Rameses II.

Philip. Son of Herod the Great.* As tetrarch he ruled areas northeast of the Sea of Galilee until his death in 34 C.E. Unlike most of the Herods, he ruled fairly. Philip has the dubious distinction of being the first Jewish ruler to mint coins with the heads of Roman emperors on them.

Pilate. The Prefect, or Roman governor, of Judea from 26-36 C.E., during the time of Jesus. (Sometimes also called the procurator, but that term actually was not used until several years later.) He set up Roman banners in Jerusalem, antagonizing the Jewish people, but reneged under pressure. In general, he had a reputation as a cruel and weak-principled leader. It is reported that he was forced to commit suicide between 37 and 41 C.E.

Sanhedrin. The "Supreme Court" of the Jewish people

(sometimes it refers to any court). By tradition it originated with the seventy elders who were with Moses; but the title "Sanhedrin" was not actually used till the close of the first century B.C.E. The court met in Jerusalem and consisted of both Sadducees and Pharisees. It had a wide range of judicial powers, both civil and criminal, though ultimately subject to Rome's intervention. After the end of the Second Commonwealth in 70 C.E., the Sanhedrin was replaced by the Beth Din.

Septuagint. A Greek translation of the Tanach* made in the third and second centuries B.C.E. The name "Septuagint" derives from a legend that 72 elders came from Jerusalem to Alexandria in Egypt to translate the Bible ("sept-" being a Greek prefix meaning "seven"). The accuracy and style of the translation are variable. The Septuagint was *the* Bible for countless Jews in the Diaspora by the last decades of the Second Commonwealth. Its significance in Messianic prophecy is that it shows the common understanding of the Messianic passages in the centuries preceding the time of Jesus.

Shavuot. Called in Greek "Pentecost," this holiday commemorates the harvest time and in Jewish tradition, the giving of the Torah on Mt. Sinai. It occurs in May or June. The Christian holiday of Pentecost is based on Shavuot.

Sukkot. A holiday occurring in September or October commemorating the booths in which the Israelites dwelt in the wilderness. Elaborate ceremonies developed in the time of the Second Temple involving water libations. Today booths are still built and the traditional lulav and etrog (willow-myrtle-palm branches and citron) are employed.

Tanach. The Hebrew Bible. The word is an acronym for

*T*orah,* *N*evi'im* (Prophets), and *K*etuvim* (Writings), the three traditional divisions of the Hebrew Scriptures.

Targum. An ancient Aramaic paraphrase of the Hebrew Bible. It became customary in synagogues to follow the reading of the Torah* with an Aramaic interpretation, Aramaic being the daily language. Originally the Targumim were oral. Of the many surviving Targumim, Targum Onkelos (on the Torah), Targum Jonathan (Prophets) and Targum Pseudo-Jonathan (Torah) are the best known, Onkelos adhering the closest to the original text.

Tetrarch. Literally, "a ruler of a fourth part" of territory, which was its original meaning among the Greeks. The Romans used it of a ruler of any part of an Oriental province. In Luke 3:1, Antipas,* Philip,* and Lysanias functioned as tetrarchs.

Torah. The five books of Moses, which comprise the first division of the Hebrew Scriptures. Usually translated "law," a better rendition would be "teaching." For a listing of its contents, see Appendix 8.

Ur of the Chaldees. The home city of Abraham, which he left to travel to Haran. It is generally thought that the modern site of Tell el-Muqayyar in South Iraq corresponds to ancient Ur. "The Chaldees" is another word for the Babylonians.

Bibliography

BOOKS BY OR ABOUT JEWISH CHRISTIANS

Buksbazen, Victor. *The Gospel in the Feasts of Israel.* Fort Washington, Penn.: Christian Literature Crusade, 1954.

Einspruch, Henry, and Einspruch, Marie, eds. *The Ox . . . The Ass . . . The Oyster.* Baltimore: The Lederer Foundation, 1975.

Einspruch, Henry, ed. *Raisins and Almonds.* Baltimore: The Lederer Foundation, 1967.

_____. *Would I? Would You?* Baltimore: The Lederer Foundation, 1970.

Einspruch, M.G., ed. *A Way in the Wilderness,* Baltimore: The Lederer Foundation, 1981.

Friedman, Bob. *What's a Nice Jewish Boy Like You Doing in the First Baptist Church?* Glendale, Calif.: Regal, 1972.

Fruchtenbaum, Arnold G. *Hebrew Christianity: Its Theology, History, and Philosophy.* Grand Rapids: Baker, 1974.

_____. *Jesus Was a Jew.* Nashville: Broadman, 1974.

Frydland, Rachmiel. *When Being Jewish Was a Crime.* Nashville: Thomas Nelson, 1978.

Jocz, Jakob. *The Jewish People and Jesus Christ.* 3d. ed. Grand Rapids: Baker, 1979.

_____. *The Jewish People and Jesus Christ After Auschwitz.* Grand Rapids: Baker, 1981.

Kac, Arthur W. *The Messianic Hope.* Grand Rapids: Baker, 1975.

Levitt, Zola. *Confessions of a Contemporary Jew.* Wheaton, Ill.: Tyndale, 1975.

Levitt, Zola, and McGann, Dr. D. *How Did a Fat, Balding, Middle-Aged Jew Like You Become a Jesus Freak?* Wheaton, Ill.: Tyndale, 1974.

Rosen, Ceil, and Rosen, Moishe. *Christ in the Passover.* Chicago: Moody, 1978.

Schaeffer, Edith. *Christianity Is Jewish.* Wheaton, Ill.: Tyndale, 1975.

Schlamm, Vera, and Friedman, Bob. *Pursued.* Glendale, Calif.: Regal, 1972.

RABBINIC INTERPRETATION OF MESSIANIC PROPHECIES

Levey, Samson H. *The Messiah: An Aramaic Interpretation; The Messianic Exegesis of the Targums.* Cincinnati: Hebrew Union College Jewish Institute of Religion, 1974.

Patai, Raphael. *The Messiah Texts.* New York: Avon, 1979.

HISTORICAL EVIDENCE FOR THE RELIABILITY OF THE BIBLE

Bruce, F. F. *Jesus and Christian Origins Outside the New Testament.* Grand Rapids: Eerdmans, 1974.

_____. *The New Testament Documents: Are They Reliable?* 5th ed. Downers Grove, Ill.: Inter-Varsity, 1960.

Cassuto, U. *The Documentary Hypothesis.* Translated by Israel Abrahams. Berkeley, Calif.: Magnes, 1961.

Kitchen, Kenneth A. *Ancient Orient and Old Testament.* Downers Grove, Ill.: Inter-Varsity, 1966.

_____. *The Bible in Its World.* Downers Grove, Ill.: Inter-Varsity, 1977.

McDowell, Josh. *Evidence That Demands a Verdict.* Arrowhead Springs, Calif.: Campus Crusade for Christ, 1972.

_____. *More Evidence That Demands a Verdict.* Arrowhead Springs, Calif.: Campus Crusade for Christ, 1975.

Morrison, Frank. *Who Moved the Stone?* Downers Grove, Ill.: Inter-Varsity, 1958.

THE RELEVANCE OF BIBLICAL FAITH TO PHILOSOPHY AND CULTURE

Chapman, Colin. *Christianity on Trial.* Wheaton, Ill.: Tyndale, 1975.

Guiness, Os. *The Dust of Death.* Downers Grove, Ill.: Inter-Varsity, 1973.

Lewis, C. S. *Mere Christianity.* New York: Macmillan, 1952.

_____. *Miracles.* New York: Macmillan, 1963.

_____. *The Problem of Pain.* New York: Macmillan, 1962.

Pinnock, Clark. *Reason Enough.* Downers Grove, Ill.: Inter-Varsity, 1980.

Schaeffer, Francis A. *The God Who Is There.* Downers Grove, Ill.: Inter-Varsity, 1967.

Sire, James. *The Universe Next Door.* Downers Grove, Ill.: Inter-Varsity, 1976.

We are eager to help both Jews and Gentiles enter the salvation and joy that come through Y'shua. For more information or help with specific problems and questions, write to:

Jews for Jesus
60 Haight St.
San Francisco, California 94102

General Index
(Subjects, Persons, Places)

Index of Scripture References

(does not include Appendix 5)

Index of Hebrew Terms

Index of Rabbinic Sources